Pores Deep

~-~

Exuding a Pleasant Fragrance or a
Malodorous Stench

M. Maynard, Ph. D.

Truth Serum
Publications

Truth Serum
Publications
OHIO

Unless otherwise indicated, all Scripture quotations are from the King James Version of the Holy Bible.
Scripture quotations marked (NIV) are from the Holy Bible, New International Version, © 1973, 1978, 1984 by the International Bible Society. Used by permission of Zondervan.
All Rights Reserved.

Truth Serum Publications
P.O. Box 201006
Cleveland, OH 44120 USA
www.truthserumpublications.com

Pores Deep
Copyright © 2012 by Truth Serum Publications,
ISBN 978-0-9839280-0-3

Library of Congress Control Number: 2011937104

All rights reserved. No part of this publication may be reproduced, stored in a retrieval system, or transmitted in any form or by any means – electronic, mechanical, photocopy, recording, or any other – except for brief quotations in printed reviews, without the prior permission in writing from the publisher. Printed in the United States of America

DEDICATION

To My Parents

Mr. James Grant Jr.
&
The late Mrs. Margaret Henry-Watson

I thank God for the parents I was blessed with. I recognize the full worth of the lessons they taught me which have made me appreciate all things great and small. I thank them for their numerous sacrifices and living exemplary lives that helped shape my character.

Dad you possess outstanding qualities that are beyond admirable. You are positively absolutely awesome! I love you to pieces.

Mom I miss you, your laugh and your dimples when you smile. I know your safe within God's arms.

Honor thy father and thy mother: that thy days may be long upon the land which the Lord thy God giveth thee.
Exodus 20:12

-CONTENTS-

Acknowledgments   1
Prologue   3

1. Beyond the Surface   5

2. Outer Court to the Inner Court   13

3. The Anointing   25

4. Don't Cast Your Pearls to Swine   35

5. An Unfathomable Stink   49

6. Dead Things Produce   61

7. Armored for Warfare   77

8. A Sweet Aroma   89

Notes   101

-ACKNOWLEDGMENTS-

To The Master Potter in Whose Hands I am Clay I say Thank You Heavenly Father. I am Nothing Without You.
To My Spouse C. Maynard: I Thank God for you. You have been an irreplaceable friend and lifetime partner, Thanks for always supporting my dreams and goals and providing whatever is needed to see them come to past. Thank you for all your support in every way. I love you.
To My Children & Grand-Daughter Michael Andrew Graddick Jr. (Millz McFly), Corey Maynard Jr., Jaera Faith Maynard and Heaven Nevaeh Graddick: Each of you have caused a cosmic shift in my destiny to do better to be better. I'm eternally grateful for the joy you continually bring to my life.
To My loving Brothers and Sister Derrick (Marvelous) Watson, Michael Washington, and Dr. Luneed Washington-Charvis: Our mother was favored among women to bring forth the four of us. I love you guys; words are insufficient to express how eternally grateful I am that you're my siblings.
To My Grandmothers, Reverend Thelma Grant & Mother Luneed Moore: Thank you for the planted seed (The Word of God) all your love, much encouragement and your Effectual Prayers that through the years has availed much.
To My Uncle Apostle Levi Henry: Thank you for the encouragement. Your 2007 Prophetic Word has come to past. The second book is already in process for release. The double portion!
To My BFF's Antoinette Clay, Cornelia A. Smith, Annjeannetta Young-Edwards and Ayamah Thompson: Thanks for always supporting whatever I want to do and

you know that's always something. I praise God for your commitment. Thank you for assisting, listening, encouraging, and the list of things you continually do.

To Dr. Caswell Morgan: Thank you for always encouraging, motivating and supporting the ministry that God has placed within me. You have always exemplified a Spirit of Excellence in the things of God.

To Dr. Richard Eberiga: Thank you for every Prophetic Word you've spoken in my life, many that have already been made manifest. You exemplify True Prophetic Ministry and a Spirit of Excellence. Thank you for Encouraging, Motivating and supporting the ministry that God has placed within me.

To Evangelist Alisa Davis, Evangelist Ena Davis, Pastor Rickey Adams and the Gospel Family: For all of your continual prayers. True Intercessors with Power!

To Aliece Stewart and Minister Cynthia Wilcox: Thank you for editing and proof reading your time and effort was invaluable.

To all My Family and Friends: To list you all there isn't sufficient space. It doesn't change the fact that I love and thank God for each of you. Especially, Auntie Louise Akins, Jerry Akins, Sylvia Durham, Florence Maynard, Dawn Maynard, Dorsey Charvis, Auntie Ann Sandridge, Leeansley Sandridge and Dr. Delores Lundy who gave an assignment that turned into a published book. I thank God for every person that gave encouragement regarding this project it has been priceless.

Eternally Grateful,

M. Maynard

-PROLOGUE-

This book has been designed to take you on a spiritual journey that encourages you to live a life that is a sweet and pleasant aroma in the nostrils of a loving God. It is a body of work that is metaphorical in nature yet, distinctively sound. Its purpose is to be informative and provide you with food for thought, causing you to delve into the wonderful spiritual abyss of holy living. I hope it will enhance your spiritual eye to see beyond what is surface.

It is imperative as a believer in the body of Christ that we seek to live an exemplary life. It should be one that is continually purified and cleansed by the washing of the word. When we are distracted and unguarded we cannot be alert watchmen on our towers and sin will look to adhere to us like glue. In the film Spider Man III, there was a villain named Venom. Venom's sinful thoughts and deceitful ways allowed a gooey black substance which was evil in nature called symbioses; to take over his body, thoughts and actions. The symbiosis is a fictional extraterrestrial parasite. The substance draws its strength from evil desires and intent. Since it is amorphous it envelopes whatever it sticks to. It inflicts a hostile takeover and is not satisfied with a little bit but desires the entire individual just like satan. In the hidden areas invisible to the natural eye, lies the possibility of sin sticking and causing foul scents to surface from the layers below. We must be ever conscious of satanic devices and the little sins that easily beset us.

The scripture clarifies in Romans 6:23 that the end result of sin is death. There is nothing pleasant about death. The very process that the body goes through produces a malodorous stench. The contents of this book it is not meant to shock or offend. We will look at a variety of subject matter from bugs to animals that produce smell in addition to the human body that produces odor in death as well as in life. You may find some things very descriptive or morbidly graphic when relating to death and the stench it produces. We all know it is necessary for every person to cleanse themselves regularly to rid the body of various germs, dead cells and odors. No one wants to be noticed or identified by foul body odor. What about our actions, temperaments and attitudes? We should consider their language carefully and be mindful that they too produce a plethora of unsavory odors.

God's love for you can conquer anything you're currently facing. God desires to have a relationship with you that will revive, rejuvenate and renew your life. He wants to transform each of us into the Godly character that is a sweet aroma unto His nostrils. Rather you're a freshman, sophomore, junior, senior or long time veteran in Christ the process is continual as we are ushered from Glory to Glory. I whole heartedly; pray this book has an effectual reaction that delivers and causes change. If only one reader is changed in any way for the Glory of Jesus Christ then I have been successful on this journey and my efforts have not been in vain.

Please note in regards to grammatical structure certain words have been deliberately capitalized and some deliberately left lowercase to place emphasis or lack thereof.

-Chapter One-

Beyond The Surface

What is meant by the title pores deep? It means going beyond that which is surface. It requires you to go beyond the various layers of our human flesh that can be visibly seen, and reach areas that require microscopic view. Many of the things being presented will need to become pictorial in your mind. You will find that many of the natural things discussed are to be applied spiritually and may require the pulling back of the Epidermis one sub-layer at a time. As you embark on this journey, remember the great adage; "As it is in the natural so it is in the spiritual."

There are so many things happening deep under the surface of our skin. We have various layers that supply much needed protection. I believe the desire that drives people to appear that they have it all together is indicative of the happenings below the surface of our human emotions. It makes many go to great length to put on facades. If the facade was an Igloo it would surely begin to melt due to the change of temperature. If the facade was an orange and we tried to remove the peeling we would find it was simply a plastic replica as it had the look but no fruit. If the facade was the brick house occupied by the three little pigs, surely it would begin to crumble with the force of a strong wind causing a shift in the bricks called life, and the big bad wolf (Satan) would make his way in. Each of these scenarios when weighed on the scale of human emotions, which can range from jolly to fickle, has the possibility of producing a pleasant fragrance or a malodorous stench.

** THE SKIN YOU ARE IN **

"I will praise thee; for I am fearfully and wonderfully made: marvelous are thy works; and that my soul knoweth right well"
Psalms 139:14

I find the human body to be extremely fascinating. It is God's creation and because He is the greatest artist it is so complex in design. It is intricate in every detail. It is so perplexed that there is no studious source of doctors or scientists that can fully understand its vast mysteries. The human body is one of the greatest machines in operation. There is no single or group source that can do justice to its multiple parts. We are indeed fearfully and wonderfully made. Absolute amazement never ceases to overtake me when reading about the human body.

While recently taking a course in human biology, I learned so much information about the human body and its many complex systems. There are several such as the skeletal, muscular, nervous, hormonal, circulatory, digestive, respiratory, reproductive, excretory and integumentary (Skin) systems to name a few. These various systems make up a composite whole. They all work together giving men, women and children the ability to maintain every aspect of human living. Each system is very interesting in its study, but my focus in this chapter will primarily be on the integumentary (skin) system and the Kardia which is the Greek term for heart. The heart is the most important muscle in the body it is also a complex organ that has multiple functions. The heart beats approximately thirty eight million times a day. Isn't that amazing? We should be so careful to take good care of it in every aspect.

> *"Above all else, guard your heart for everything you do flows from it."*
> *Proverbs 4:23 (NIV)*

The heart is the centre of all physical and spiritual life. 1 It is the sustainer of life itself. Without its operation we as humans cease to exist. It is identified as "The fountain and seat of our thoughts, passions, desires, and appetites". 2 The heart is the core of our affections, purposes, and endeavors of human understanding. The scripture above clearly indicates that everything we do flows from it. Through God's divine design joined to our soul, the heart is the faculty and seat of one's will, one's intelligence and one's character.

** UNDERSTANDING YOUR PORES **

"Wisdom is the principle thing; therefore get wisdom: and with all thy getting get understanding"
Proverbs 4:7

PORES DEEP

The human skin has several million pores and associated glands covering the surface of the skin. Pores play a very important role in the overall function of our skin and the health of our bodies. A section of your skin about the size of a quarter has approximately six hundred sweat glands. Pores are tiny holes that act as outlets for sweat and sebum to leave the body. Our skin consists of three layers: the epidermis which is the thinnest and outermost layer of our skin, the dermis; is where we find the sweat glands and hair follicles and many nerve endings, and the hypodermis, which is the innermost layer of our skin.

As we go beyond the surface we find beneath the layers, glands that play a primary role in the body's temperature regulation. Sweat glands, are quite numerous and are present in all regions of skin. When the body temperature starts to rise, sweat glands become active. 3There are two types of sweat glands. There are ordinary eccrine sweat glands that are found over most of the body. They produce sweat that exits through the skin pores but this sweat is not offensive or foul smelling. The second type of sweat gland is the large apocrine sweat glands found in auxiliary, pubic and perianal regions. The apocrine sweat glands have a more limited distribution, but are found in some of the following areas:

Axilla (underarm), Perianal (rectal area)
Areole (nipple), Periumbilical (around the belly button)
External ear canal, Genital area

BEYOND THE SURFACE

There is no known function attributed to apocrine sweat glands in humans. However, when it comes to the composition of the apocrine sweat glands it is clear that bacterial decomposition leads to odor. The stench varies from person to person some more pungent than others. Without question the majority of these areas listed above are private in nature. Sin can be very private; it can be masked very well. It can be so faint that one can't smell the tinge of bacterial decomposition. It's not until it begins to surface; meaning it has already taken a foot hold can a stench of odor be detected. The length in which the stench remains unaddressed determines how loud it gets. There is no doubt that the smell will become more fetid with time.

"If you do what is right, will you not be accepted? But if you do not do what is right, sin is crouching at your door; it desires to have you, but you must rule over it."
Genesis 4:7(NIV)

Sweat in and of itself has no odor. The smelly effect that it has is the fault of the apocrine glands that are located in the groin, armpits and other hairy body parts. The bacteria colonies in these warm, moist areas metabolize and create the foul smells. So I would say that sin in itself does not have an odor. The reeking putrid smell is produced by dabbling in it. Its musty stench is developed by putting it into action. The longer you dabble, the greater the stench which allows demonic strongholds to metabolize and build colonies. This allows sin to fester in the hidden areas of your heart creating a mephitic soul which is full of odor.

** DOES YOUR FLESH DIE DAILY **

Yes, it surely does though you may not feel it or actually see it. Dead skin cells are a form of bodily waste that facilitates the growth of new epidermal cells. Every minute, you lose about thirty thousand to forty thousand dead skin cells. These are all replaced immediately by fresh skin tissue. Your body sloughs off dead skin cells through normal daily activity. The body that God has given us is a teacher. It is showing us by example the importance of dying to our flesh daily to "slough it off". Follow this simple lesson taught by the skin you're in. Rid yourself of frustration, worry, bitterness, envy, and strife. An essential means of a healthy transformation is the renewal of our minds. We have to be changed in our thinking and remove ourselves from the old things because they have the ability to corrupt us if we allow them to.

"22 You were taught, with regard to your former way of life, to put off your old self, which is being corrupted by its deceitful desires;23 to be made new in the attitude of your minds; 24 and to put on the new self, created to be like God in true righteousness and holiness."
Ephesians 4:22-24

How are we supposed to do that? We have to take it one day at a time. Each day should begin with being washed in the word. This gives God the lead in the start of our day. The Christian walk is progressive, like a fruit it becomes ripened with time. This progressive walk has no end as long as we are in the earth realm. We continue to strive each day to be better, to do better. We should perform continual self-examinations no matter how sure we are of ourselves concerning this perfecting progression. It is imperative that we do not to lean to our own understanding but in all of our ways we should acknowledge God. He is the only absolute of perfection. With this in mind we won't take for granted the valuable lesson taught by the skin we are in. It lays a visible foundation and proves that we should, we ought and we must die daily. There has to be regular Bible reading, application of what has been read, prayer and fasting. This is of the utmost importance in being built up in the things that will keep us grounded and produce a pleasant fragrance in the nostrils of God. This is a sure preventive measure of exuding a malodorous stench.

-Chapter Two-

Outer Court To The Inner Court

There is a wise proverb that says "Beauty is only skin deep." When traced back it is first found in a work by Sir Thomas Overbury in 1613. Mr. Overbury's rendition says "All the carnal beauty of my wife is but skin deep." It is simply saying that outer beauty is not always what it appears to be and what matters is something far deeper. Preferably what is deeper is something that is very good but the truth is that it could also be very bad. We live in a society where people are consumed by the appearance of things. They are drawn by the lust of the eye. Doesn't sound like anything too new does it? Adam and Eve's fall in the Garden of Eden came because of the lust of the eye, the lust of the flesh, and the pride of life. The lust of the eye can be very subtle. It has the ability to lead to what I've decided to call the quintuplet D's which are "distract, divert, debilitate, defeat and destroy"1 the noblest of people. Beauty is in the eye of the beholder but we all want to behold and have that which is beautiful. We all desire to be fabulous, to be gorgeous, and attractive. The question is at what cost?

"Watch and pray so that you will not fall into temptation. The spirit is willing, but the flesh is weak."
Matthew 26:41(NIV)

PORES DEEP
.................μγμ........................

** NEXT TOP MODEL **

Today we see an overwhelming increase in cosmetic procedures of all kind. This ever growing industry has become a fourteen billion dollar business. There are some people who have become addicted to plastic surgery. How do you become addicted to plastic surgery? I don't think I will ever fully understand or know. The pain, the swelling and the long weeks of recovery; I will say no more. Yet the sum of money being spent is staggering. I've seen sudden changes in the appearance of some Tele-Evangelists as well. Yes, many Christian brothers and sisters are having cosmetic surgery done that removes and add to and from their person. Apparently some do not like their chins. Someone else may not like a cheek bone and who knows what else. They seek to change their outer appearance when maybe it is their internal parts that need surgery of a different kind. The world is filled with many beautiful people as we look upon the top layers of the skin. Ooh, but when we go beneath the surface, when we go pores deep we will discover a chamber of rotting corpses. Their attitudes are putrid in essence; their arrogance is rancid and crawling with maggots. Their outer houses are magnificent but their inward parts are full of dead men bones.

"Vanity of vanities", saith the Preacher vanity of vanities;
all is vanity.
Ecclesiastes 1:2

I can't tell others how to live their lives and I'm not trying to sit in the judgment seat. I do understand that the same measure in which I judge I shall be judged. Nevertheless, I don't see scripture that validates having plastic surgery for vain fancies. I believe that various circumstances carry choices that are personal. I know that cosmetic surgery is broad so I will narrow it down a bit. I'm talking about taking pieces off and putting pieces on. Stuffing pieces and doing all matters of sorts with pieces; until some pieces get smaller and some get bigger. I think that about sums it up. The ways of the world are a snare to us. That is why we have to come into relationship with God so that we can move from the outer court into the inner court. Reading and getting an understanding of the scriptures will educate us on what is right or wrong concerning our personal choices. It is through daily prayer that we develop our personal relationship with God. It is through this relationship with Him we are able to make better choices that will produce a pleasant fragrance.

"Finally brethren, whatsoever things are true, whatsoever things are honest, whatsoever things are just, whatsoever things are pure, whatsoever things are lovely, whatsoever things are of good report; if there be any virtue, and there be praise, think on these things."
Philippians 4:8

When we think of true beauty without question our purveyor of pulchritude is Christ. There was no one else qualified to meet the substantial need of the human plight. His beauty and moral excellence is grandeur beyond compare. For there is nothing in which to make the comparison. I know you've heard the saying "Setting the Bar high", He is the bar! He is greatness in epic proportions. His name is above every name.

> *"9 Wherefore God also hath highly exalted him, and given him a name, which is above every name: 10 That at the name of Jesus every knee should bow, of things in heaven, and things in earth, and things under the earth; 11 And that every tongue should confess that Jesus Christ is Lord, to the glory of God the Father."*
> *Philippians 2:9-11*

** ELOHIM'S MASTERPIECE **

To be like Elohim, this is the beauty man should strive for; to walk in the masterpiece image of the Lord Jesus Christ becoming aromatic sweetness. The example and layout of the Tabernacle also called the Tabernacle in the wilderness was an early foretelling of Christ. It is a picture perfect layout that shows us the way to Christ and true worship. This is what leads to that which is pleasing to God. It produces a sweet and pleasant fragrance. The Tabernacle was a place constructed to meet a holy pattern, designed to meet a holy purpose, that we could go into God's holy presence. The gate was and is the only way of access.

"I am the Gate; Whoever enters through me will be saved. He will come in and go out and find pasture"
John 10:9 (NIV)

Christ is the one and only way to our Heavenly Father, Christ and Christ alone is the gateway there is no other entry.

Jesus answered, "I am the way and the truth and the life. No one comes to the Father except through me"
John 14:6 (NIV)

Understanding the significance of the Tabernacle is important in understanding the work of Jesus Christ on the Cross. It is only by entering through the gate that a person could receive forgiveness of sin by offering up sacrifices upon the brazen altar. The brazen altar was used to place the burning animal sacrifices upon it. This was the first step in approaching a holy God because the blood of an innocent animal had to trade places with a guilty man. The blood of the animal was a temporary atonement for man.

"For the life of a creature is in the blood, and I have given it to you to make atonement for yourselves on the altar; it is the blood that makes atonement for one's life."
Leviticus 17:11(NIV)

These sacrifices had to be performed annually. An animal's blood could not adequately atone for man permanently to satisfying the demand sin had created. Jesus Christ who is the Lamb of God was the ultimate sacrifice.

> *"10 By the which we are sanctified through the offering of the body of Jesus Christ once for all. 11 And every priest standeth daily ministering and offering oftentimes the same sacrifices, which can never take away sins: 12 But this man, after he had offered one sacrifice for sins forever, sat down on the right hand of God; 13 From henceforth expecting till his enemies be made his footstool. 14 For by one offering he hath perfected forever them that are sanctified." "18 Now where remission of these is, there is no more offering for sin."*
> *Hebrews 10:10-14, 18*

I have stated prior that we should be continually cleansed by the washing of the word. In the tabernacle we now come to the laver which was located between the brazen alter and the holy place. This laver reminds us that we need cleansing of all unrighteousness before we attempt to approach a holy God. After the priests atoned for the sins of Israel they were required to wash themselves in the laver before entering and serving in the holy place. If they did not do so they would die. We too need to bathe in the laver of the word of God. It is this continual washing process in the word of God which keeps us from dying spiritually and having a malodorous stench of decay. Christ is the living word; He is the Logos, the written word made manifest. When we give our lives to Christ we are covered by his blood. God no longer sees our spots and blemishes of sin anymore but the precious blood of Christ. Our daily intake of the word cleanses us so we can serve and be fit for the master's use.

> *"25 ... Christ also loved the church, and gave himself for it; 26 That he might sanctify and cleanse it with the washing of water by the word, 27 That he might present it to himself a glorious church, not having spot, or wrinkle, or any such thing; but that it should be holy and without blemish".*
> *Ephesians 5:25-27*

After washing in the laver the priests entered into the Holy Place. Inside the Holy Place was the "golden lamp stand". The priests were instructed to keep the lamps burning continuously. This lamp stand was the only source of light and represents Jesus as the only true light of God. The "table of showbread" was also located in this area and held 12 loaves of bread. Only priests could eat the bread and it had to be eaten in the holy place because it was considered holy and set apart. A "fragrance of freshly baked bread topped with frankincense filled the holy place"[1] what a pleasant aroma indeed. This was to show forth Christ as the bread of life.

"I am the bread of life. He who comes to me will never go hungry, and he who believes in me will never be thirsty."
John 6:35

It is this wonderful bread that we symbolically eat during communion to remember that He has given His body for us. What have you given to Him? Have you given your life to Christ? Decisions can sometimes be difficult and can produce a variety of results. I testify assuredly that giving my life to Christ has been the greatest decision I have ever made. Every man, woman, boy and girl are called to live a life that is a sweet and pleasant aroma to God. There is no human being in the earth realm that is excluded. We can be the nicest of people and not have anything we believe would be ungodly in our lives. There are many people who do not drink, smoke, or anything that is unseemly but it doesn't mean anything if we have not given our lives to Christ. He is knocking at your door this very moment. Open the door and let Him in and tell Him from your lips to His ears "Jesus I surrender all unto you".

"20 Behold, I stand at the door, and knock: if any man hear my voice, and open the door, I will come in to him, and sup with him, and he with me. 21 To him that overcometh will I

grant to sit with me in my throne, even as I also overcame, and am set down with my father in his throne."
Revelation 3:20-21

As we continue to move from the outer court into the inner court we are still making our way inside of the holy place. We now come to "The golden altar of incense", which sat in front of the curtain that separated the holy place from the holy of holies. Incense was burnt on this altar continually. The incense represents our prayers and intercession of God's people going up to God as a sweet fragrance. The Golden altar represents Christ our intercessor who continuously intercedes on our behalf. He continually makes intercession for the saints.

"3 And another angel came and stood at the altar, having a golden censor; and there was given unto him much incense, that he should offer it with the prayers of all the saints upon the golden altar which was before the throne. 4 And the smoke of the incense, which came with the prayers of the saints, ascended up before God out of the angel's hand"
Revelation 8:3-4

We finally come into the "Most holy place" also known as the holiest of all. Only the high priest could enter this room during the appointed time. This was God's dwelling place He appeared as a cloud by day and a pillar of fire by night above the most holy place. The curtain that separated the "holy place" from the "most holy place" was called the veil. The "most holy place was the immediate presence chamber of Jehovah". 2 There was only a piece of furniture inside called the Ark of the Covenant in which the Mercy Seat rested. Inside of the ark were the tables of the law, a golden pot with manna, and the budded rod of Aaron. The high priest entered this area only on the Day of Atonement which took place annually. Before entering the most holy place the priest, took great care and tedious preparation. If anything was done out of order by a fraction he would drop dead in the most holy place. Bells were on his garments to hear him move about and the people attached a string to his garments to be able to pull him out if he died inside. The presence of God engulfed this room and anything that was contrary to holiness; His Spirit would move upon destroying it instantly. This is only a light summary of the tabernacle. I pray it will give you a desire to study and learn more about it and the word of God. II Timothy 2:15 states that we should study to show ourselves approved. In this we will be able to rightly divide the word for ourselves. As you look at the layout of the Tabernacle you see the importance of moving from the outer court into the inner court. The further in you go the greater the presence of God you will find. Relationship is built through progressive movement.

It is absolutely necessary that every born again believer understand the act of Christ upon the cross. It is when Christ's blood hit the mercy seat that the veil was torn and God's presence became accessible to all. The redemptive plan of God for man was complete. This is His act of

Agape love; the perfect love story, a true romance. God loves us so much; how much more should we desire to praise Him and lift Him up. It is what we were created for. It is what we were created to do. In our progression from the outer court to the inner court we forge the development of a personal relationship. It brings the dawn of a new day, opening our understanding and clearly making known the knowledge of Christ and who we are in Him. When we become full of Christ, our pores can only exude that which is redolent of the incense burned in the Tabernacle, a sweet and pleasant aroma.

-Chapter Three-

The Anointing

"But the anointing which ye have received of him abideth in you, and ye need not that any man teach you: but as the same anointing teacheth you of all things, and is truth, and is no lie, and even as it hath taught you, ye shall abide in him."
1 John 2:27

What is the anointing? The anointing of God is given through the Holy Spirit that takes residence on the inside. This allows us to operate effectively in the things God has created us to carry out. Every born again believer has a divine purpose. We are all responsible for sharing the things that we know concerning our savior with those who He places in our sphere of influence. The anointing of God is divine power from on high. We do not operate in our own strength but it is of Gods power and His alone. Our lives should be ambrosial in nature exemplifying a spirit of excellence in the things of God. Devotion for God is the pathway to the power of the anointing. Devotion is an intense in depth fellowship beyond what is mediocre. It builds up and produces a personal relationship. It is private; it is your secret place and it should become distinctively aromatic. It isn't your will that you seek but the will of our Lord. It isn't any act that we can carry out it is simply one's state of mind "Set your mind on things above, not on earthly things." (Colossians 3:2 NIV) Our minds are to be stayed on him in the sense that we seek to please Him in every way. When we understand who we are and whose we are there is no longer a worry about if God will perform what He has spoken. It is a faith walk that acknowledges; that God is omnipotent. (All Powerful) He is the creator of everything in the universe and beyond. Without God nothing is possible but with God all things are possible. The anointing is granted to those who dwell in the secret place of the Most High. Do you qualify? You don't have to be a preacher, teacher, prophet or have a title to qualify. You simply have to have a true thirst after God one that develops a personal relationship.

"Thou wilt keep him in perfect peace, whose mind is stayed on thee: because he trusteth in thee."
Isaiah 26:3

** GOD WANTS YOUR HEART **

Desire is not enough to qualify for the anointing. The anointing will cost you something. There isn't any how to remedies that can qualify one for the anointing it is a process. The anointing is acquired by committing the desire of your heart to God in exchange for Gods best. Our lives should be sold out for Christ it's like that beautiful song titled. "I give myself away." by William McDowell There is a complete surrender because we have come to a place of resolve to trust him totally. We come to know God with our heart but we show our true love for him by the way that we live. Through this surrendering process we become a usable vessel whose pores are exuding that which is fragrant.

I'm reminded of the story of David; the bible declares that he was a man after God's own heart. Eliab, Abinadab and Shammah were three of David's oldest brothers. They are actually the only brothers that were acknowledged by name as they passed before Samuel when he was sent to anoint the one God had chosen king. (I Samuel Chapter 16) We find that David was not present though all of the other sons were. One would tend to think that David should have been present in the room since the request was that all of the sons be brought before Samuel. It was only after God did not choose any of those considered as fine choices by man standards was David summoned directly by God. That is good food for thought. It doesn't matter what people think about you. It's about what God thinks about you. The most beautiful can be so superficial. Indeed "Beauty is only skin deep." God was looking far deeper than surface pores. David's brothers appealed to the eye but lacked the internal components. In other words its apparent that though David's brothers had the look just like a plastic orange they had no fruit!

"12 So he sent and bought him in. Now he was ruddy, with beautiful eyes and a handsome appearance. And the Lord said, "Arise anoint him; for this is he." 13 Then Samuel

took the horn of oil and anointed him in the midst of his brothers; and the Spirit of the Lord came mightily upon David from that day forward. And Samuel arose and went to Ramah"
1 Samuel 16:12-13

God gives the anointing to those who are committed to doing His will and to those who are willing to allow their lives to bring Him glory. God's anointing is available to those who have a heart to seek to know His heart. David's siblings didn't have the measure found in him. After David was anointed he went right back to his previous job description. He didn't boast and brag he simply remained humble. David still had the heart of a servant. He had a heart that could be trusted to give God the glory. David pores exuded an aromatic pleasantry that pleased God.

Now getting back to the brothers acknowledge by name Eliab, Abinadab and Shammah they were all a part of the Israelite army that fought against the Philistines and big bad Goliath. These soldiers were all trembling in their boots when they heard the threats of Goliath. As the younger generation would put it "Goliath had them shook". The bible says that for forty days Goliath heckled and taunted the Israelites. David went to the battle ground not as a soldier but as a servant; an errand runner to be exact. David was taking food to his siblings at the request of his father. Goliath appeared as he had several times before and

THE ANOINTING

insulted the Israelites and invited any man to fight him one on one. No one had taken a stance for fear.

> *"And all the men of Israel when they saw the man, fled from him, and were sore afraid."*
> *I Samuel 17:24*

David wanted to know who this wretched fleabag who hadn't even been circumcised was. Who was this Philistine that dared talk the kind of trash talking Goliath did. David enquired what will be done for the man that will seal his pie hole. David's brother Eliab became indignant when he raised the question. Now don't be shocked that's just like people, church folk included, they were fine till you decided to do something bold and different. David had only come to bring food to put in his brothers ungrateful belly. Saul was told about David's statements and his boldness. It was at that moment David had been summoned before the king. David said he had no problem fighting the Philistine. Despite Saul's warning to David that he was only a youth and unequipped to handle this mighty giant of war who was a warrior from his youth, David did not back down. To sum the story up quickly David killed Goliath. He defeated this giant without any armor. That is correct this little fellow used only a sling and a stone. Once he slew Goliath he beheaded the giant with his own sword. David was able to do this thing because he depended solely on the Lord. David was endowed with power from on high which allowed him to do the impossible. It was not David's strength and power but he walked and trusted in the strength and power of an amazing God. David was a friend of God and because of their relationship God was able to entrust David with the anointing.

> *"45 Then said David to the Philistine, Thou comest to me with a sword, and with a spear, and with a shield; but I come to thee in the name of the Lord of hosts, the God of the armies of Israel, whom thou has defied. 46 This day will the Lord deliver thee into mine hand; and I will smite thee, and take thine head from thee; and I will give the carcasses of the host of the Philistines this day unto the fowls of the air, and to the wild beasts of the earth; that all the earth may know that there is a God in Israel."*
> *I Samuel 17:45-46*

** ANOINTING FALL ON ME **

The pouring of oil in the Old Testament signified the anointing of the Holy Spirit being smeared on a chosen vessel. After Christ ascended to the right hand of the father and the day of Pentecost had come the Holy Spirit was granted access to reside in the believer. Jesus Christ was anointed with the Holy Spirit in the New Testament as an example to us today that we need the anointing in our lives to be affective witnesses and effective in our perspective offices and callings. We must be able to identify the voice of God before we can fully operate in His anointing power.

THE ANOINTING

Would you trust a stranger with your most valuable treasure? You have to abide in the presence of God to acquire a greater anointing. There are many who argue that there are different degrees of the anointing. I'll simply say everyone doesn't have the same power though the same power through Christ is available.

> *"Verily, verily I say unto you, he that believeth on me, the works that I do shall he do also; and greater works than these shall he do; because I go to my father."*
> John 14:12

In essence what I'm saying is "different strokes for different folks." Some people press into God with greater desire and zeal than others. There will always be born again believers who are just happy to be saved. They are satisfied with being in the number one more time. The anointing rests in them to keep them from falling, but they are not looking for an anointing like Elijah or desiring the double portion of the anointing like Elisha when he received the Mantle of Elijah. (*II Kings chapter 2*) A strong anointing is the greatest recipe for living effectively and powerfully especially in the times we reside in today

** MANTLE ANYONE? **

"A time will come when instead of shepherds feeding the sheep; the church will have clowns entertaining the goats."
C.H. Spurgeon

Today we find a church house full of those interested in wearing a title but have not possessed a mantle. A mantle is a spiritual garment provided by God that covers and envelops you with power to do great exploits. This spiritual garment adds some super to your natural. However, with all of the robes and fine garments we see on leaders today many think a mantle is simply a purchased robe or attire. Many have gone out to department stores and purchased their Sunday's best. They mistakenly thought that would suffice; a store bought suit or robe is not a mantle though it may look good it lacks the anointing. A mantle is tailored made by the master and is endowed with power! In the kingdom storehouse your money is no good as Christ has already paid the price. You can financially bless the preacher but he can't qualify you for the mantle or give you an anointing. In order to get the mantle you have to go to the fabric store called Jesus and only the Holy Ghost is qualified to sew the pattern. Just like in the intricate details of the Tabernacle of Moses; a mantle has a specified pattern and no man is to deviate from the layout. You can only wear the suit you were designed to wear. We live in a day and age where there are ministry leaders who are seminarians who have more degrees than a thermometer. They have come to feel that the degrees have qualified them and they are operating in their gifts but are mantle less! They have head knowledge but no anointing. They are the "You Think I'm Powerful and So Do I Generation" they have no relationship, let alone power to assist a dying generation.

THE ANOINTING

"Having a form of Godliness, but denying the power thereof: from such turn away."
II Timothy 3:5

Perpetrators and imitators replicate what they see who is going to press the olives? Who's looking for the Holy Spirit of God to give them a mantle saturated with the anointing? Will it be you? It comes at great cost you must endure the test and trials that come to make you strong. The anointing will not hang out with the flesh. Your flesh has to be fully submitted to God and must be crucified daily. Ask God to search the heart and remove any wicked thing. God is looking for a vessel that is pure. Once tested by the jeweler gold plated jewelry will never pass as twenty four carat gold. Many may already have relationship with God and may very well be anointed. However, I want you to think about the levels of the anointing; what if they were gold carats 10, 14, 18, or 24 which carat would you be? Continue to press, God is not through with you yet you always have room to be better because in God you have the ability to be platinum! Let your aroma be platinum.

"But He knows the way that I take; when He has tested me, I will come forth as gold."
Job 23:10

-Chapter Four-

Don't Cast Your Pearls To Swine

There are many idioms ascribed to our pork belly friend called the pig, more negative than positive. Some can make you chuckle and there are those that can cause offence. The response of the idiom would depend on the one you use, and the context in which you use it. The outcome can even spark a little controversy. Our first African American President Barak Obama discovered that during his historic Presidential run. He unintentionally offended the Republican runners John McCain and Sarah Paline with the line "You can put lipstick on a pig, it's still a pig." President Obama's camp said he didn't mean it to imply anything negative but Mc Cain's camp demanded an apology. As my friend Annjeannetta would say "Got to be more careful." In presenting this chapter I will do my best in being careful not to sugarcoat the truth as I do not wish to be offering up any apologies. This is not a carnal segment in the book it's about the stench of carnality and the truth of the matter is quite foul.

** PIGGY AT A GLANCE **

"The pig is also unclean; although it has a split hoof, it does not chew the cud. You are not to eat their meat or touch their carcasses."
Deuteronomy 14:8(NIV)

PORES DEEP
....................μγμ........................

The pig has been biblically identified as unclean because although it has a split hoof similar to the cow and appears outwardly clean internally his digestive tract does not operate the same; this is what causes the animal to be unclean. The pig not chewing the cud simply means he has a stomach more similar to humans. We have one stomach but a monogastric digestive system which is singular in nature. Wherein, the cow has one stomach but a polygastric digestive system that has four different compartments, so it's plural in nature. This allows for a greater breakdown of their food as it returns back through the first stomach to the mouth again to be chewed a second time.

Like the pig you may have been born monogastric in the natural but in Christ you can be born again in the spirit and be made polygastric. If you don't chew the cud in the spirit you can find yourself like the pig unclean lacking understanding and discipline in the Word. However when you are born again and made polygastric you can regurgitate the word of God over and over again. The born again believer can be cleansed over and over again. This will enlighten the believer and assist them in avoiding all things that are defiling and vile. Which digestive system is currently operating inside of you? Ponder that; Christianity today has become so inclusive you can't tell the "Aint's" from the "Saint's" because the "Saint's" keep fluctuating between systems. Either you are ruminant or not; either you are meditative and contemplative or not. Do you meditate on the word of God day and night? Do you contemplate your course of action? Do you dip or sit in the cleansing fountain of the Word? To be redolent with the aroma of Holiness you'll be required to sit for a lifetime no dipping allowed.

** CAN YOU CLEAN UP THIS PIGSTY? **

If we used a scale we would have a tilted balance between those who believe pigs are filthy animals and those who believe they are clean. Some say pigs actually prefer being in a clean environment. I read that they keep their toilets far from their living and eating quarters and even piglets only a few hours old will leave the nest to relieve themselves. Those who have studied and have raised pigs say that they are very intelligent and quick learning animals. Outside of what is said of them scripturally the fact is that pigs are omnivorous feeders. In a nutshell they eat whatever is available. I am sure on that note we can agree their diet is horrific. They will eat any and all kind of excreted matter. I am referring to pigs outside of piggeries though it happens there too.

Piggeries are farms and factory farms where domestic pigs are raised. The pig is also considered very dirty because they roll around in the mud. However, I read pigs roll in mud not because they can't get enough of it, but because they have ineffective sweat glands. It's said the pig rolls in the mud and the dried layers of mud protect their skin from sun burn and helps keep them cool. Maybe their keepers do not keep their corners tidy and the pig is identified as dirty due to no fault of his own. Some would say that given proper space and someone who will clean up consistently after the pig we probably would not find the pig to be as nasty as we have come to believe he is. I have reviewed the arguments and I would repeat the idiom used by the President of this great Nation "You can put lipstick on a pig, it's still a pig." Barak Obama

** FLUCTUATING SMELLS **

Bona fide Christianity always exudes a pleasant aroma. It never makes room for stale air it always envelopes it. This scented fragrance can only engulf a room through a true relationship with Jesus Christ on an intimate and personal level. Universally a pleasant fragrance is always preferred over a malodorous stench. We can find ourselves surrounded by innumerable odors on a daily basis. We smell different foods that can cause our stomachs to growl and have our tongues salivating with great anticipation. We may encounter perfumes or colognes that can cause you to feel nauseated. Depending on where you work you may encounter odors of a stronger and far different kind. In the Hospital you may smell the stench of illness or if you work in the mortuary the unpleasant stench of death. Olfaction is the sense of smell. Smell often identifies the presence or absence of odor rather than quantifies its intensity. Our ability to perceive odor varies from person to person.

In a study on odor perception it was identified that "Infants appear to like all classes of odorous materials." and that "Children younger than five years old rated sweat and feces as pleasant."[1] The study also found "odor fatigue occurs when total adaptation to a particular odor has occurred through prolonged exposure." [2] Odor adaptation simply put is becoming accustomed to an odor. In other words the person has been in the stink for so long they have lost all sense of smell. Ever visited someone's home that had a dog or cat and it made their home smell bad? Yet everyone that lived there could not tell there was a fungus among us. Like the perception of smell varies from person to person so does the degree of a person's likes and dislikes of certain smells. So the stench of sin may be more than you or I can bear but for other's due to prolonged exposure they have odor fatigue and no longer have the ability to detect its presence. New babes in Christ can't yet decipher, and babes being weaned still can't smell distinctively! Lord help us.

** TO MARKET TO BUY A FAT PIG **

Many aspiring entrepreneurs want to open up their own piggeries. There are also larger factory farms called Intensive-Piggeries that raise pigs as well as slaughter them for profit. Piggeries are all around the world from the United States all the way to Uganda. There are even how to guides in starting piggeries. Wow, Pigs are big business, pigs rake in filthy money no wonder they are called dirty. The communities in which they operate are crying for help and want to shut each and every one of them down indefinitely. The people who live close to these locations can barely stand to breath the stench on these farms. The smell is a great displeasure to the families in these communities. The fecal matter and other sewage cause a ferocious stench, one not to be reckoned with. The fecal matter is so poignant because the pigs manure has ammonia, phosphorus, and hydrogen sulphide which, smells like rotten eggs. This is all mixed with other matter, need I say more. That sounds like a very wicked potion. It may also be putting the people that live near these farms in harm's way health wise. The U.S. government thought it serious enough that they are shelling out over one million dollars in grants. The study is for the management of swine odor and waste.

Now from a spiritual window I think we would do well to study how to manage swine odor and waste in the church, the work place, community centers or even the supermarkets where pigs should be in ready to buy packaging. We too should be able to ban together on a united front to keep them from gathering in droves in the pews, the office and the checkout lines. We may have to deal with them when they are first ushered in or newly hired but we shouldn't have to live with them as they are because change is supposed to come.

> *"Therefore if any man be in Christ, he is a new creature: old things are passed away; behold, all things are become new."*
> *2 Corinthians 5:17*

We all are unclean before we give our lives over but remember through Christ we receive an internal cleansing to be made whole. We come in monogastric and by the power of the Holy Spirit are made polygastric. The swine mentality and omnivorous actions should not stay the same until we have them duplicating by the thousands in one place; the stench would be unbearable and holiness demands that it has got to go. I'm sure you have sat with, talked to, and even hugged quite a few oink oinks in the building. Some have not been dealt with or corrected so they have developed fraternities within the church, the work place, or a locality near you. The name of their universal chapter is Phi -Iota- Gamma- Sigma. Those are Greek letters for P-I-G-S. This stands for Perpetrating Intentional Grace Sliding. Have you been initiated? Have you taken the pledge? I'm sure at one time or another especially as babes lacking knowledge every one of us almost signed up. We are called to walk in grace not slide in and out of it. I know a reader just fell off their chair and yelled blasphemous! I suggest to that reader you go back to the prologue which is the introduction of this book and read that some things I say are metaphorical. Get up, relax and finish reading. I am referring to those who proclaim Christ. We as Christians should be a sweet fragrance in and out of church. There cannot be any straddling the fence.

"1 As for you, you were dead in your transgressions and sins, 2 in which you used to live when you followed the ways of this world and of the ruler of the kingdom of the air, the spirit who is now at work in those who are disobedient. 3 All of us also lived among them at one time, gratifying the cravings of our flesh and followings its desires and thoughts. Like the rest, we were by nature deserving of wrath. 4 But because of his great love for us, God, who is rich in mercy, 5 made us alive with Christ even when we were dead in transgressions it is by grace you have been saved. 6 And God raised us up with Christ and seated us with him in heavenly realms in Christ Jesus, 7 In order that in the coming ages he might show the incomparable riches of his grace, expressed in his kindness to us in Christ Jesus. 8 For it is by grace you have been saved, through faith and this is not from yourselves, it is the gift of God."
Ephesians 2:1-8

** THE TWELVE TRIBES OF PIGITES **

The love of God in our lives produces an insuppressible aromatic odor that consumes one's surroundings. There can be no denying by anyone who comes in contact with those who are fully submitted and walk in the true knowledge of Christ that they have been changed. They come out of the pigs den and cut their selves loose and walk away from their kinsman. In Genesis chapter 12 God told Abraham to leave his family and friends to travel to a new place. He took him out of Haran being without an heir to become the father of nations. This is what change and obedience can produce; today because of Abram's close encounter with God we can now say that we are the seed of Abraham. Sometimes you have to walk away from close friends and family to walk out our destiny. Don't be discouraged Abraham is your example that sometimes you have to leave an old thing to receive the new. Abraham also is a testament that the new supersedes everything the old had to offer.

Do not be alarmed but when you become a born again believer this very action in itself will make many people walk away from you. This is all for your good, there are also a few omnivorous creatures you must depart from and leave behind of your own free will. The twelve tribes of pigites are a developed secret society and when you meet them its like "Buying a pig in a poke" as my father would say. He used to hear that from his grandfather. It always makes me laugh when he says it. It's an idiom that means committing yourself to something without carefully inspecting it first. (In order to verify that it actually is what it was described as being.)

The Twelve Tribes Consist Of:

The Piglites – They love to roll in mess (1 Tim. 5:13)
The Snoutites – Their always sniffing out mess (Prov. 16:27)
The Oinkites – Their always talking mess (Prov. 18:8)
The Hoofites – Their always walking in mess (James 3:10)
The Pigtailites – Their Talebearers of mess (Lev. 19:16)
The Pigearites – They love to hear mess (Prov. 25:28)
The Hamhockites – Of close relation to the Hoofites but their one notch above the hoof literally, the sedity high steppers they dip in mess. (Prov. 14:16)
The Ribites – They are more commonly in a group or found in "Racks" and you will never find them without a "Spare" rib their sidekick, they stay in a variety of mess and can always be found at Barbeques. (2 Thess. 3:11)
The Hamites – They are neutral to mess. They are "Real Hams" always presenting the perfect cover. (Prov. 20:23)
The Baconites – They dabble in slices of mess. They love small settings like the breakfast table. (Prov. 16:28)
The Porkites – They fit the full embodiment of the swine. They are one notch above the Chitterlingites they bathe in mess (2 Cor. 12:20)

The Chitterlingites – They've fallen and can't get up out of their mess. They can't see the error of their ways. They're looking to bring all the pigs into the parlor. (Rom. 1:29-30)

** YOUR PEARLRIFIC! **

"Do not give dogs what is sacred; do not throw your pearls to pigs. If you do, they may trample them under their feet, and then turn and tear you to pieces."
Matthew 7:6 (NIV)

You are a pearl a rare gem; do not cast your pearls to swine because they do not know, nor do they comprehend true value. The twelve tribes of Pigites are not able to appreciate a pearl and can't understand respectably how to embrace what is different. When you allow the Holy Spirit to make a deposit and bring forth change your extraordinarily rare. The Pigites had the ability to be a pearl but decided a cubic ziconia was far easier. It allows them to remain who they are denying the power therein. They are satisfied with the false appearance of being good stock. They can only assist you in becoming ensnared and bound. Do not muddle with them as you'll find yourself empty and in want. In Christ you have power to negate the tactics of the enemy who seeks to put you in a stronghold. "It doesn't matter where you start it matters where you end." If you find yourself ensnared remember Christ came to set the captive free.

PORES DEEP
....................μγμ........................

"So if the Son sets you free, you will be free in deed."
John 8:36 (NIV)

Return to your first love; if you haven't received Christ yet don't delay, do it today. All you have to do this very moment if you are not saved is ask God to take over as your Lord and Savior. Ask for forgiveness of every sin you have ever committed. Ask God to let the Holy Spirit take residence on the inside of you to lead and guide you into all truth. Confess with your mouth that you believe God raised His Son Jesus Christ from the dead and He now sits in heavenly places as your advocate. Ask and believe these things and you shall be saved. Instantly at that very moment of believing and asking from the true depths of your heart you will be transformed from darkness into the marvelous light.

Now you are pearlrific, an added jewel to the body of Christ. A harvested pearl in the kingdom of God that is as unique and individual as a fingerprint; God's design is of the strictest standards. You are a pearl with great luster, luster is the amount of light a pearl reflects both from its surface glow and its inner light, continue to search yourself often. As you walk with Christ your surface with smooth out. Subtle blemishes and tiny marks are part of any pearl's natural texture and proof of its genuine origin. Fewer surface imperfections denote a higher quality, a more valuable pearl. This perfection does not come by grinding out scratches with the buffer you bought but through Christ's perfecting power. It's His redemptive blood that has made your surface appear flawless to an omnipotent God.

In researching the value of pearls I discovered that the Nacre is the iridescent internal layer. This is one of the most important aspects of pearl quality because a pearl with thin nacre will not last. Nacre is the natural substance produced by mollusks to make pearls. The twelve tribes of pigites layers are thin therefore they are easily drawn back to the lusts of their flesh. A pearl with thin nacre, while often blemish free, will typically have a chalky or dull appearance having no value because the Holy Spirit is not allowed to operate He is quenched by their choices.

> "Quench not the Spirit"
> 1 Thessalonians 5:18

The Holy Spirit literally sets the standard for grading the quality of a pearl. The Holy Spirit sets the bar and illustrates unadulterated perfection to the system, with triple-A representing the very highest quality. The Spirit of Christ is the only factor that can represent the true worth of a pearl, as he magnifies the luster and buffs our surfaces to perfection. It is in Christ and in Him only that we can meet the standards of spiritual excellence. There is wonder working power in the blood of the lamb. Christian pearls are truly natural gems. They are not cut, dyed, altered by heat but perfected by the refiner's fire. The luster of a pearl is the measure of its awesome brilliance and reflectivity. People should be able to see the reflection of Christ in you. God is coming back for a church that is without spot or blemish. In Christ our surface is without bumps, discolorations, and is totally shiny and reflective of our maker. He will smooth us out and make us perfectly rounded in Him. Perfectly rounded pearls are indeed extremely rare and the most expensive so in Christ you are pearlrificly priceless! So know your worth and do not cast your pearls to malodorous swine.

-Chapter Five-

An Unfathomable Stink

"Oh, my offence is rank it smells to heaven"
Shakespeare

There are some odors that are so repulsive that there is no articulate way to rightfully describe the malodorous turbulence it brings to a room or location. This very same repulsion initiated by that stench is what a Holy God feels concerning all sin that mankind engages in. Just as darkness is uncovered by light, the stench of sin is uncovered by holiness. The only thing that can wash away sin is "The blood, the blood, the blood" of Jesus. After we give our lives to Christ we are also required to refrain from doing things that can so easily tangle us up again. It would not be wise for a cigarette smoker to have a carton of cigarettes sitting on their nightstand if their trying to be rid of this filthy habit. I remember over twenty years ago being delivered from cigarettes. I had to make a decision to trust God to deliver me. Some people may have experienced overnight success. It took me weeks because I first tried to do it myself. I smoked Newport's so I decreased to Newport lights then I started to Salem because I thought they were even lighter. It wasn't until I began to cry out to God to deliver me and ask Him to remove the need, the desire, and the urge was I set free instantly. I haven't looked back since. It's amazing how I acknowledge the stench of a cigarette smoker today. I can't believe I once

PORES DEEP
. . . . .μγμ . . . .

smelled that way. I was a walking puffing stink bug well, maybe not that malodorous.

The true stink bug has an unfathomable stink; they are from the family of pentatomidae and belong to the order of hemiptera .The unique feature of the hemiptera is its mouth. It looks like a beak and has the ability to pierce tissues (plant tissue) they exude a foul smelling substance from their pores located on each side of their thorax. They also have the ability to create large populations. Pause. That should be a pretty scary thought. The stink bug sucks plant juices and damage crop production. They are resistant to many pesticides they don't die they multiply. In some of the species their liquid contains cyanide compounds. You are aware that cyanide can be and is deadly. Some of the species can be found in the common household down in the basement. This group is called water bugs but the more predatory ones are called the water scorpions. There are some which are skin crawling parasites too, like bed bugs and kissing bugs, do tell.

Let's walk on the spiritual side of that. We can find stink bugs all over the place. Sounds like anybody, I meant any bug that you know? They have the ability to produce large populations or clicks. They attach themselves to new plants and suck on the plants juices. Eventually they damage the new plants view and outlook concerning the things of God. The new plant tries hard to fight its juice sucking foe with little prayer and bible reading. (this would be a pesticide)

AN UNFATHOMABLE STINK

They have not come to understand that these are their weapons in God so they lack the ability to wield their sword. Their little prayer and bible reading isn't strong enough as we have already been informed that these stink bugs are resistant to many pesticides. More prayer more power, no prayer no power! These stink bugs are located in the work place but this is to be expected because many of these environments are anti-Christ. You may find some at family gatherings pungent to the core. Depending on which stink bug one has encountered the cyanide compounds could be deadly sending anew babe in Christ back to the world. The thought is a sad one. Could this; is this happening in the church today? Are people coming through the doors of the church looking for a safe zone slaughtered at these very doors by parasites on assignment? Are lost souls turned back out to the streets without Shepherd's being aware? "Shame, Shame, Shame" yet it's the truth. So many sheep the count is astounding. Pastor Bo Peep lost his sheep but didn't know he needed to go out and find it. Was that sheep just a number on the roster? Or has the job description of a shepherd changed?

Back to the bugs, the kissing bug is a Judas' it wears two faces and can be found by the boat load what a stink they make. They create and cause mass confusion they are very cunning and appear to always be extremely peaceful. The kissing bugs colors are camouflage and they blend into their surroundings well. This critter is very hard to detect, what a commotion you'll find yourself in before you know it. Then we have the water scorpions which are venomous in the spirit realm, as they are dream killers, faith snatchers, back bitters, liars, and gossipers they aim to harm their target. They are full of the putrid stench of hate. They don't want anyone to go further than they have gone which half of the time isn't anywhere. They will infect everything that is in its company.

> *"The thief comes only to steal, kill and destroy; I come that they may have life, and have it to the full."*
> *John 10:10 (NIV)*

How is it possible to be in the house of the Lord at every service, every choir rehearsal, every meeting, and every fish fry and still be a part of the walking dead? How can you put on a facade at church and be hell on wheels the remainder of the week? When people encounter some Christians at the work place they find someone evil as a rattle snake in boots several sizes too small. If the wages of sin is death and a person walks in the fullness of sin without repentance they are dead men walking. Sin is separation from God how putrid is the house with dead corpses all over the building? There are even dead corpses standing in the pulpits not just the pews. You can read about in Church Folk Going to Hell in A Hand Basket.

> *"For the wages of sin is death, but the gift of God is eternal life in Christ Jesus our Lord."*
> *Romans 6:23*

AN UNFATHOMABLE STINK

Remember you are accountable for your actions and though it may not yet be discovered by man you can't hide from God. He is omnipresent which means He's everywhere at one time. He is omniscient which means He is all knowing. Our goal is to produce a pleasant fragrance and to depart from anything or anyone that exhibits otherwise. The devil has to try to penetrate the church, the work place, the grocery stores, the gym, the community center and anywhere else he can to keep Christians from making it into heaven. Don't be discouraged you are an over comer in Christ because you are not simply looking to be a part of a group of people in a single building. You are seeking to know an eternal God intimately so that the Church resides in you and you can walk with it everywhere you go. Upgrade your mind move past just being part of a local congregation. That's important for fellowship but understand the body of Christ is a universal connection not a building connection.

** THERE'S A FUNGUS AMONG US **

It's the mysterious case of a flower gone sour or a metamorphosis of a malodorous power. There is indeed a strange and unusual flower which blooms that has a scent not of pleasantry but a more sinister aroma one that is pungent to the core. The very name acknowledges what one become's when death finds you. It is called "The Corpse Flower" its stench is horrific. It is said this flower literally smells like decaying flesh which we will discuss in greater context in the next chapter. During pollination it attracts decaying flesh eating beetles, flies and sweat bees. The stench can be smelt 100 feet away from the greenhouse. The sad thing I discovered is that there are a few corpse flowers in the corporate office up the street in full bloom. The tolerance for dead things has become common place. So much so, that the people who should be able to detect the stench are no longer running to get the spiritual Lysol. Preferably they would use Febreze as it removes the stench and replaces it with a fragrance of pleasantry without choking you. In other words where are the Christians that have relationship with God for real? Where are the prayer warriors that can raise a dead thing in the spirit realm? Where are the Christians that can pray and change an atmosphere? Demons should be cringing in your local super market because you walked in. In the local church, who is still teaching that we must walk in holiness and believes in operating through the rod of correction willing to sit you down if you're out of order? Is there none? Is there a few? Why is that so? The news media is detecting the church's sin and showing it on the ten o'clock news on a regular basis. This is the enemy's tactic to give many unregenerate men and women reason not to want to become a part of the body of Christ.

"Foolishness is bound in the heart of a child; but the rod of correction shall drive it far from him."
Proverbs 22:15

AN UNFATHOMABLE STINK

With all of the spiritual mothers and fathers declaring they have created all of these spiritual sons and daughters whose administering spiritual spankings?

> "Whoever spares the rod hates their children, but the one who loves their children is careful to discipline them."
> Proverbs 13:24

If we walk upright and exemplify the true essence of Christ people will be drawn by the pleasant fragrance our Christianity exudes. There is always room for improvement in every person and Christ is the greatest improvement to our interior because this enhances and beautifies our exterior. Allow your aroma to be captivating and change the atmosphere. Even the corpse flowers stench is no match to overpower the pleasant fragrance of holy living!

> "If my people, which are called by my name, shall humble themselves, and pray, and seek my face, and turn from their wicked ways; then will I hear from heaven, and will forgive their sin, and will heal their land."
> 2 Chronicles 7:14

** CAN'T TOUCH THIS **

"For rebellion is like the sin of divination, and arrogance like the evil of idolatry. Because you have rejected the word of the Lord, he has rejected you as king."
I Samuel 15:23

All we have to do to ooze with a sweet fragrance is abide in the word of God. The word is renewed daily by His new mercies. We are all guaranteed to go through the various seasons of life. In our abiding in the word of God we can blossom and be in full bloom in our own seasons. We all have to go through our winter, spring, summer, and autumn. The vast array of flowers created by God has wonderful aromas and are beautiful in appearance. This is what Christians should resonate, the sheer beauty of love, peace, and joy. On the other hand you've already been informed about the copse flower pungent to the core. This we can compare to rancid pride and arrogance which are sins brooding in our times.

I now present to you another flower in full bloom in many locations called the voodoo lily this particular plant is of the aracae family and it is poisonous and smells like dead mice in a plastic bag when it blooms. I use this flower to make comparison to this rebellious generation. The word of God says rebellion is likened to witchcraft. These are the colleagues and members that can't be given instruction, they can't take constructive criticism, can't be corrected, totally lacking order and structure. Yet, they love the Lord and they were called to your church, or your organization and they intend to get their pastor or president on the right path with their new agenda. Sounds like Sister "Know It All?" Probably is, nevertheless we may have all found ourselves in a bad place at one time or another in our quest to walk upright before the Lord. Witchcraft is in bloom all

AN UNFATHOMABLE STINK

across the globe and it is not of God. A Christian should make every effort to carry out the work of our Heavenly Father. God gives power to those who believe the truth of His word. The word of God is a lamp to our feet and a light to our path. Believers and worshippers of God we must intercede for the entire body of Christ. The prayers of the righteous availeth much our prayers are sweet incense.

"Lest Satan should get an advantage of us: for we are not ignorant of his devices"
II Corinthians 2:11

Many Christians are unequipped to face the enemy called satan. They are not prepared to go into any kind of battle because they lack the depth of the word and the endurance for prayer. In order to walk in power you have to make some sacrifices. You have to sacrifice time in the realm of prayer. We have to p.u.s.h. which means "pray until something happens." There will be times when some answers to the prayers you have prayed will take great patience. The manifestation of your answers may seem like they are taking eternity to break forth because there on God's clock. He is not bound by the time of man He is outside of time. Witchcraft is a stronghold and of a demonic nature and has to be a yolk broken from on high. A Christian should seek to learn more about the discipline of fasting. The word of God makes it clear that some things we encounter in the spirit realm can only be conquered by prayer and fasting. Fasting increases your spiritual sensitivity in the realm of the spirit and draws us closer to God.

> *"And he said unto them, this kind can come forth by nothing, but by prayer and fasting"*
> *Mark 9:29*

** BEYOND HUMAN TOLERENCE **

Humans have great capacity for curiosity. Scientist are always mixing and creating all kinds of chemical substance. In human war there may be rules that have to be adhered to but in the spirit realm the enemy doesn't fight fair. Every soldier needs to be equipped for the battle because this warfare is very different. This battle is not with flesh and blood and only through relationship with Christ can you have every weapon you need and the blueprint of how to infiltrate the enemy's camp. The only objective should be walking in the victory you already possess. If you try to enter in this kind of warfare with your fist you are in for a world of trouble.

> *"The weapons we fight with are not the weapons of the world. On the contrary, they have divine power to demolish strongholds."*
> *2 Corinthians 10:4(NIV)*

AN UNFATHOMABLE STINK
.................μγμ........................

The stench of hell nauseatingly reeks of sulfur! What can be beyond human tolerance in the realm of smell? What kind of stench is unfathomable? Give me a long drum roll please… Isonatriles, these manmade concoctions are the worst of all and are called the Godzilla's of smell. isonatriles have even been patented for use as non-lethal weapons for war. Let's look at this from the spiritual side. In the spirit realm I would compare this rancid stench to the workings of witches, warlocks, and demonic activity they are making the body of Christ ill. Many Christians have been punched in the gut and are leaning over with their insides panging.

What can this be likened to in sin? I would say murderers and character assassinators. This kind of putrid odoriferous smell is hard to recover from. It is like being hit by a tractor trailer that leaves gaping wounds and body parts all over a highway. The pain of rejection, being jilted by a Christian spouse, being lied on, being spat upon, and being talked about. It doesn't kill instantly like in the natural remember Isonatriles are non-lethal weapons. However, it does come close to an attempted murder in the spirit. It is brutal because it is a slow methodical form of torture. We are battling this stench in every place imaginable it shows no love. This kind of malodorous stench is a satanic onslaught that's difficult to recover from in our own human abilities but in the spiritual realm the work of the cross has the power to alter the life of the wounded, spat upon, jilted, lied on, talked about, and the rejected. We must continue on our walk of faith knowing assuredly that the pleasant fragrance that exudes from us conquers all evil that may be sent our way. Know assuredly that in Christ we receive a sweet fragrance of deliverance that allows us to overthrow every assignment of the enemy. All praises to Jesus Christ the sweet fragrant Balm of Gilead.

"But thanks be to God, who always leads us as captives in Christ's triumphal procession and uses us to spread the aroma of the knowledge of him everywhere. For we are to God the pleasing aroma of Christ among those who are being saved and those who are perishing".
2 Corinthians 2:14-15 (NIV)

-Chapter Six-

Dead Things Produce

"Wherefore, as by one man sin entered into the world, and death by sin; and so death passed upon all men, for that all have sinned."
Romans 5:12

Death has become a natural part of life though it was not intended to be that way. This was not God's original plan for man. In the book of Genesis, we find Adam and Eve who were the first humans in the earth realm. They were given specific directives by God that were to be adhered to. They were also informed of the dire consequences that disobedience would bring. They knew no sin but through the deceit of satan and their poor choices the state of innocence was lost. Through this one act of disobedience every human fell under the curse and man became captive in a state of sin. However, God's love for us made a way that we could overcome this curse through the death, burial and resurrection of the only begotten son of the Father Jesus Christ.

"For the wages of sin is death, but the gift of God is eternal life in Christ Jesus our Lord."
Romans 6:23 (NIV)

If we live long enough we are bound to meet with death at our appointed time. From dust we were made and to the dust we shall return. It is inevitable that death will knock on our door, the door of a loved one, or someone we simply know. Even though death touches us in this manner, we yet find there is life all around us and the living must carry on. Death is never easy to accept; it can be very hard, very disturbing and very saddening. Death produces grief and mourning but with each new day we learn to cope. Death is a course of life that we cannot change in the natural. Yet, I can hear the saints say, "But God!" through the redemptive act of Christ and His shed blood we have been given the ability to change it in the spiritual.

In these modern times because of a more sophisticated and commercialized society we have been isolated from the stench of dead things. Death is a part of life in more ways than one because dead things also produce food. We have food plants and meat factories that provide our food already prepped and cleaned. Therefore, the stench of death is faint though present. Exposure is only common for those who work in a field that requires it. How many people walk up on a cow or lamb which they then slaughter for dinner that evening? Perhaps a Farmer or a person that lives in a remote location would. I'm ecstatic we can go to the grocery store and purchase an already slaughtered chicken, cow or lamb. Otherwise, I'd probably be a vegetarian; I'm sure of it.

Now from a spiritual perspective in these times the church has also become very sophisticated and modernized. This has caused a greater acceptance and tolerance of a variety

DEAD THINGS PRODUCE

of things. If I was Dorothy with my beautiful ruby slippers on the yellow brick road I'd say, 'Glamour, Splendor and Grandeur, Oh my." The stench of death is in the air. There is a stench of dead things everywhere. Dead carcasses are in the city; dead corpses are in the field. We walk over them in our coming in and we leap over them in our going out. The state of the Church today is in grave need of repair. What does glamour; splendor and grandeur have to do with a stench? It is the abundance of carnality in grand form that has swept through the modernized church like a Tsunami. This is my slice of perspective and surely there will be one sanctified Christian critic that may find this as an offense. I simply say "If for you and your house it doesn't apply let it fly." Sin is constantly expanding the grave yard it's full of dead men bones and new corpses are arriving by the boat full. To have the world is not enough satan wants the Church too. We must awake out of our slumber.

> *"If my people, which are called by my name, shall humble themselves, and pray, and seek my face, and turn from their wicked ways; then will I hear from heaven, and will forgive their sin, and will heal their land."*
> *2 Chronicles 7:14*

The Word of God makes it clear that the penalty of sin is death. Sin can be so faint, or so silent that it is deadly. Eve bit into a fruit and shared it with her husband and cost humanity everything. There was no sound except the faint whisper of her voice into her husband's ear. Sin can be silent because of the subtleness of satanic devises. If only some of us would scratch and sniff our high priced suits we may very well find they are rank from the very stench of carnality. There are others, who entire wardrobe should be sent to the cleaners in heavens court. The holiness of God is not to be approached without "kid gloves" (soft gloves made from a lamb) of sanctification. Christians are always required to lead exemplary lives of holiness like Christ. This is not an option it is a requirement.

** FEAR FACTOR **

Bishop T.D. Jakes has a video series titled "The Blood Speaks" it makes mention of the first murder in the history of mankind with siblings named Cain and Able. The blood of the slaughtered brother spoke from the ground to the creator. (Gen. 4:10) I say the blood also speaks by stench! To "speak" by definition means to communicate, signify, or disclose by any means. In society today we are slaughtering each other through word and deed. The blood is crying out from the ground. Just reading about death in detail can repel and disgust a reader. Not only does death smell bad it looks far worse. Seeing a gutted animal or corpse can be a ghastly sight. Witnessing daily shootings and bombings has to be complicated. Death on a battlefield can never become something people get used to. This is why when humans

DEAD THINGS PRODUCE

experience it in the worst way they need counseling. Some people get better over time while others never seem too fully recover. Death on a continual cycle is not what we were meant to endure, it is horrendous. Ghastly acts of slaughter leave an impression in the mind. This is why some crime scenes encountered are described as heinous or said to be un-reprehensible. Dead things can produce fear in the living. Fear has a malodorous stench of its own. It has a repelling scent like that of a skunk to keep you away from your dreams and destiny. Do not allow the stench of fear to grip and cripple you.

To give a very mild example of fear, I remember getting a job as a Veterinarian Assistant. I had no experience and was excited to have the opportunity. I remember being called into the operating room to assist the Physician with an operation for the first time on a dog that was in a grave condition. Fear punched me in the gut I had never been in an operating room before. Knowing that I have a weak stomach I began questioning can I do this? I walked in unsure of what to do. I was only required to pass the Doctor some surgical tools. I discovered the stench of illness can be very pungent. In that operating room the walls began to close in. I began to salivate and feel nauseated as the stench of the dog insides filled my nose. When I saw the internal organs it was very disturbing. I began to feel like I wouldn't last long standing on my feet it got so hot in the operating room. The Physician asked if I was feeling well, I must have appeared a bit flushed. I faintly replied yes all is well. I found myself at that moment pleading with the Lord to hold up my legs a few more minutes because the surgery was almost over. I realized that I was not cut out for being a Veterinarian Assistant but I was still proud that I took the chance. If I had not taken the chance on getting the job and stepping into that operating room I would never have known if it was for me or not. Fear is meant to stop us and hold us in our tracks. Its relationship with death is its ability to stop productivity. Do not allow the malodorous stench of fear to lock you in a box. What is holding you back or keeping you from making a new move? Change can bring a pleasant aroma to your surroundings through limitless possibilities.

We took a bit of a detour from the death of flesh to fear producing a death process. Even though the stench of fear is not as apparent as rotting flesh it still is the result of a murder. To get us back on track with the stench of death let's imagine this scene, we find a huge warehouse freezer full of meat and the power shuts down. No one is aware of the outage and the company is closed for 3 weeks. The weather is 100 degrees and rising each day. What do you imagine will happen when the manager of that warehouse returns and opens that freezer? Imagine the stench he just got socked with. What would it take to remove the odor and how long would it take to remove it? This is the way our lives would be if Christ hadn't paid the price on the cross for our sins. We would be carcasses of rotting flesh trapped in a hot box. (Hell) Thank God for His electrifying power

DEAD THINGS PRODUCE

to keep the power on in our warehouses! He has all power in His hands, the power to preserve rotting meat in the warehouses of life. He has all power to raise a dead corpse on the battlefield called life.

> *40 Then Jesus said, "Did I not tell you that if you believe, you will see the glory of God? 41 So they took away the stone. Then Jesus looked up and said, "Father, I thank you that you have heard me. 42 I knew that you always hear me, but I said this for the benefit of the people standing here, that they may believe that you sent me." 43When he had said this, Jesus called in a loud voice, "Lazarus, come out!" 44 The dead man came out, his hands and feet wrapped with stripes of linen, and a cloth around his face. Jesus said to them, "Take off the grave clothes and let him go"*
> *John 11:40-43(NIV)*

The death of Lazarus was purposed to show us the power of an omnipotent God. When Christ speaks whatever he has spoken is made manifest. He had to call Lazarus by name because if He had simply said "Dead arise everything at that time in the cemetery would have gotten up. That's Power! He can speak to every dead area of your life that is producing a stench of decay. All you have to do is open the door to your heart and He will gently and kindly come in and fill every room with the aroma of restoration. What a pleasant fragrance that is in the nostril of God. It is not His Will that any man should perish. So hear the voice of the

Lord concerning your situation. Come out of the tomb and take off your grave clothes!

** DETERIORATING CIRCUMSTANCES **

Now we will go hard core concerning the truth of death. It is a fact that a dead lifeless body undergoes a deteriorating process called decomposition. Death is "A permanent cessation of all vital functions: the end of life."[1]

Once the brain and heart shut down every other function of the body ceases to operate. All the muscles in the body relaxes this is called "primary flaccidity" where the muscles and limbs fall flat and sometimes cause involuntary stool and urine passage. This brings forth odor at the onset, the body then goes through a cooling down period and bacteria inside continues to work. It devours the human flesh it once was designed to protect. This transition is called autolysis, or self digestion. The body then enters the stage called rigor mortis where the entire body becomes rigid and stiff. The muscles are unable to relax now, so the joints become fixed in place. This process can last between one to three days.

Putrefaction certainly is the least pleasant stage of the decomposition process. This creates a lot of chemical gases like hydrogen sulphide and methane. They produce a "rotten egg" odor. The gas and bacteria cause a greenish

DEAD THINGS PRODUCE

discoloration of the skin and it begins to darken. After several days, insect larvae may begin to crawl out of the body if they have had access to it and soon flies begin to show up. Gases produced by bacterial and chemical processes begin to cause the body to bloat. The stomach becomes rounded and puffed up. The eyes may begin to bulge out, the tongue may protrude, and the pressure continues to surmount within the body and will begin to seep out. If the description is gross can you imagine the stench?

In the advanced stage of decay also called black putrefaction the body's internal organs begin to liquefy. The putrefying liquid comes from the mouth, nose, or any other opening. The stench from the rotting body can be and is overwhelmingly powerful, if within an enclosed space. It is in this stage the body bursts open under pressure, spilling its contents. The bloated stomach has eventually collapsed and the flesh has become creamy like cottage cheese. The exposed parts of the body have turned black. Insects and mites are enjoying the body pretty good. However, if insect don't have access the bacteria is still at work and will continue to consume the flesh. Reeking liquids sink into whatever is under the body. It tends to fall apart easily. The skin is not only loose but gooey. This is known as the "skin slip". Because the epidermis just slips off. The thin outer layer of the skin sloughs right off. The hair is loose, and if you jiggle the nails and teeth, they will come out easily. In this stage the body is a very messy vile pile.

PORES DEEP

The body then enters what is called the fermentation stage where it smells like cheese. This is caused by butyric acid, this happens around the time when the body starts to become dried out. Mold will form where the body lay. It is now "rotting" away. The smell isn't as putrid as before and over time the body enters the skeletal stage. Unlike the flesh bones can take years, decades, even centuries to decompose. The bones can last almost indefinitely.

Like decaying skeletal bones sin has been in the earth realm for centuries and will remain until the day of Christ's return. There are massive bodies decomposing in the earth. We live in a dying world and we have been mandated to reach them with the gospel. What will you do to rid the world of decomposing souls and the stench of rotting corpses? How will you bring the pleasant aroma of Christ to a dead area or a valley of dry bones in these end times? Do you walk in the power of the Lord to prophesy like Ezekiel to the dry bones and command them to live? (Ezekiel 37) Let us tell the lost about a Savior who can change the stench of death to a pleasant fragrance that exudes the sweet scent of perfume.

"Go ye therefore, and teach all nations, baptizing them in the name of the Father, and the Son and the Holy Spirit."
Matthew 28:19

DEAD THINGS PRODUCE
. . . . .μγμ. . . . .

** IT EATS THE DEAD **

A fly can be very annoying the buzzing sound it makes as it continues to circle, can drive you bonkers. I bet what you didn't know is that a fly can eat well on a dead body and lay up to three hundred eggs upon it that will hatch within a day. The larvae that emerge from the eggs are extremely efficient flesh eaters. Starting on the outside of the body where they hatch, maggots use mouth hooks to scoop up the fluids oozing out of a dead body. A first stage larva is about two millimeters long at the start but by the time it finishes it may be as large as twenty millimeters long. Maggots can consume up to sixty percent of a human body within days. Maggots are something dead things produce. I remember seeing maggots as a kid in a garbage can. I have even seen them on rotting food. That did not prepare me however for the encounter I later had with maggots in my young adulthood.

There were two people I knew fairly well that were heroin addicts. Their addiction was far gone and had caused them both to have a limp when they walked from shooting heroin in their groin area. Person A's lower leg formed a sore that began to smell like rotting flesh. Soon maggots appeared in the decaying area. Person A was also ostracized because of their stench and literally slept on the top steps in an apartment building leading to the roof. It was unbelievable to actually see maggots on their flesh. No one could endure person A in their presence long because of the odor. Person B soon met a similar fate of an open sore forming on their hand and maggots eating at the flesh. Both succumbed to death over a period of time. I didn't know that maggots could reside on a living being and their body could have a dead area that was a feast to these flesh eaters! These were kind people who were loved by many but their choices consumed them to death in the natural. Are your choices allowing maggots to feast on you in the spirit realm? Are you decaying day by day in various areas of your spiritual life? Are you being ostracized because of your malodorous stench? The scriptures have proven that Christ is a restorer and he can speak to a dead thing and it must rise. He has the ability to call a dead rotting corpse from the tomb and call it by name to come forth. We revisit Lazarus who was deceased and Christ called him after he had been dead for four days. We have learned that this is the time in which the body goes through a variety of changes and the odor is ferociously pungent. Sin produces changes in our lives that make us repelling to a God that wants to love us. Holiness cleanses the stench of our decay. Let's continue to ask the Lord to wash us over and over again. Let us ask God to saturate us with His presence and to cleanse us with hyssop. Hyssop produces a minty scent a fragrance that represents and signifies cleanliness.

"Cleanse me with hyssop, and I will be clean; wash me, and I will be whiter than snow."
Psalm 51:7 (NIV)

DEAD THINGS PRODUCE
.....................μγμ.......................

** BENJAMIN'S, GREENBACKS, MOOLAH **

Death has become a multi- billion dollar business. The Funeral Industry alone is making an eleven billion dollar profit. It currently costs more to die today than it costs to lease a car for 3 years and I'm not talking about a luxury car. Dead things produce monetary gain for the living. The things happening at funerals and after them are getting more and more bizarre. Dead people can be found standing up, some can be found riding motorcycles into the afterlife literally. You can get a tricked out casket covered with thousands of cubic zirconia's if you can't afford diamond chips. You can even have a diamond ring or necklace made out of your loved ones cremated remains. If you would like you can have their remains orbited around the earth. Today you can pick, choose and refuse the way you would like others to remember your earthly end.

At the Funeral Parlor up the road "Morticia" the Mortician is very skilled at her craft. She has two humps on her back and a missing eye, six teeth and a crooked smile. She can't beautify herself but she can do wonders for the dead. She'll make a dead person "look like they were just sleeping." The funeral may be the final curtain in the natural but in the spiritual you'll be returning to your maker and that's where we truly begin. Some will rest well until the day of Christ's return. Then suddenly, they will hear the sound of the trumpet and be caught up. Those who didn't get a chance to go with that group can rest assure there is another. The second group will be led down what we will simply call "The eternal death row" with shackles. Eternal damnation shall surely be their plight.

An outwardly display of perfection for the length of a funeral service may portray that they were laid to rest well. However, one cannot mask their ending in the spiritual; the display will be eternal darkness. Full of embalming fluid the stench of decay is hidden in the coffin. Time isn't on their side as they enter the depth of the pit called the grave. Their flesh which has been hidden under garments will become infested with maggots that will feast on the rotting corpse and eat down to the bone marrow. Make a choice today, we are free will agents and can choose either life or death. Death leaves a malodorous stench that repels but life produces an aroma that is pleasantly magnetic. My prayer is that you will choose life and the life in you will shine so brightly causing others to follow that magnetic glow. Share what you know and tell others about Jesus the true light that can give them life. The blessing of being a Christian is we are the living. We know that we shall die the physical death yet remain forever alive. The course of those who reject Christ remain in the state of the dead. They walk daily amongst those of us who are living and think they will die upon the physical death when they have been dead all along.

DEAD THINGS PRODUCE

"14 For we believe that Jesus died and rose again, and so we believe that God will bring with Jesus those who have fallen asleep in him. 15 According to the Lord's word, we tell you that we who are still alive, who are left until the coming of the Lord, will certainly not precede those who have fallen asleep. 16 For the Lord himself will come down from heaven, with a loud command, with the voice of the Archangel and with the trumpet call of God, and the dead in Christ will rise first. 17 After that, we who are still alive and are left will be caught up together with them in the clouds to meet the Lord in the air. And so we will be with the Lord forever."
I Thessalonians 4:14-17 (NIV)

-Chapter Seven-

Armored For Warfare

"Power tends to corrupt and absolute power corrupts absolutely" John Dahlberg-Acton

There is a raging war, an infamous battle that is continually taking place. Indeed, there are natural wars occurring around the world but the war I'm referring to is one invisible to the human eye. This is an active ongoing war in the spiritual realm. The dark side main objective is to pollute. We are in the center of this battle daily. This is not something new we have already discussed that sin came into existence during the fall of mankind. This warfare agent is so intertwined and woven in the fabric of our society that we can often walk through its doors without warning. Its hospitable manner is so inviting. Only keen perception to smell can detect its poisonous deadly stench. Rather we are conscious of it in our surroundings or not a war is being fought at all time.

In The above quote Mr. Acton was referring to the power man has been entrusted to carry out by other men without an overseer. Like a police officer having the authority to enforce the law or the power of a judge to sentence a person to twenty five years or imprisonment or for life. The power of sin is far greater than this. It is a Power that has had a hold on the morality of every man since Adam that passed through the womb. No man except Jesus Christ could and did conquer it. In Him only are we over comers.

** KNOW YOUR POSITION **

A spiritual warrior sits upon the watchtower and looks for signs of the enemy from afar. We must study our enemy to know who they are and their tactics. We should first decipher what is their method of attack. What kind of weapons do they have? Are they suited with any armor? What are their strengths and their weakness? How can we rightly prepare to win a war and be ignorant of our foe? Knowing our enemy is extremely important. However, knowing whose army we are in and the position we hold is far more significant. How can you win a war and you don't know who you are? We must know the proper armor and how to wear it. We must learn our spiritual trade tools and through practice become skilled workers. In our human frailty we must lean on God to help secure our fortresses. When you know that God is for you and He is more than the world against you who can defeat you? In knowing Christ in His fullness we come to understand the arsenal of weapons in our tool belt and can properly plan our defense though Christ. It is through practice that we come to know our position under an omnipotent God.

"13 Therefore take up the whole armor of God, that you may be able to withstand in the evil day, and having done all, to stand. 14 Stand therefore, having girded your waist with truth, having put on the breastplate of righteousness, 15 and having shod your feet with the preparation of the

gospel of peace; 16 Above all, taking the shield of faith with which you will be able to quench all the fiery darts of the wicked one. 17 And take the helmet of salvation, and the sword of the spirit, which is the word of God."
Ephesians 6:13-17

** KNOW YOUR WEAPONRY **

Every believer must know in order to stand against the wiles of the devil we first have to be able to protect ourselves. God has given us defensive and offensive weapons to use against our enemy. Ephesians 6:13-17 lists six individual pieces. We are informed of the necessity to take up the whole armor. The whole suit is required to endure and overcome the dangers that we face.

The Belt of Truth
The belt was worn by Roman soldiers to help secure their weapons and loose fitting garments. The belt assisted in keeping their clothes and belongings intact. This assisted the soldier in being more effective and swifter in running. In its spiritual application the power of God's truth makes us free from all forms of bondage the enemy tries to entangle us in through deceit and lies. God's word is truth and it sanctifies and sets us apart. (John 17:17)

The Breastplate of Righteousness
The breastplate was worn to protect the soldier's vital organs. It covered from the neck down to the waist. In its

spiritual application this means being in a condition that is acceptable and agreeable to God. Meeting the condition comes through operating in integrity, virtue, rightness and purity in the things of God. This condition is only attainable through our faith through Christ by His shed blood being our covering. (Philippians 3:8-9)

The Shoes of the Gospel of Peace

Roman soldiers wore special sandals that had nails embedded in them to provide the soldier the ability to stand firmly. In its spiritual application we are to walk in and stand on the peace that we have in God. We should be prepared to stand firm on the word no matter what is happening under the surface of our feet. Rain, sleet or snow can change the stability of our walk depending on the shoe we wear in the natural as it can get a little slippery at times. The shoes God is providing are solid through all seasons. (Psalms 119:165)

The Shield of Faith

Soldiers carried individual shields that protected them from the fiery arrows of attacking enemies. The shield could also be used offensively to push back or to knock the opponent down if they were to close. In the spiritual it is imperative to understand that faith has to be our absolute resolve. We can't waiver in the faith we must know that Jesus is our provider, protector, buckler and our true shield from all manifestations of evil. And if the enemy has gotten too close to us in his onslaught, know that by using faith in

Jesus our shield we can knock him back and strike him with a deadly blow. (Mark 9:23)

Helmet of Salvation
A Soldier wore helmets to protect their heads from being struck with an arrow or sword. The helmets were made with metal plates inside to provide less chance of a head injury. In its spiritual application one must be aware that satan cannot force us to sin but he can try to persuade us. The battles frontline is in the mind through planting false doctrine, Carnal interests and all manner of deceit. We must protect our minds at all time. We must not allow our minds to become enslaved to sin. A single thrust to the mind is a devastating blow and recovery varies in degree and eternal death is a possibility if God's word does not become engraved in our minds. (Hebrew 10:16)

Sword of the Spirit
The soldier's offensive weapon is the Word of God. In its spiritual application every believer must use the logos (written word) and the rhema (spoken word) of God with great precision and accuracy. We are to study the word of God this enables us to rightly divide the word of truth. And like the literal embodiment of the logos (Jesus) you can defeat wound and kill the enemy. (Hebrew 4:12)

Jesus Christ is our full armor. He is in every detail of the gear we should dress in daily as we proceed into battle.

After the victory which is guaranteed we can bask in His glory as sweet incense unto His nostrils during the victory parade.

** READJUST YOUR SUIT AS NEEDED **

From the very moment we are conceived a battle is set in motion. A constant struggle wages for the life within the womb. I believe for God chasers the pressure of the battle is far more severe. The enemy is always looking to steal and conquer our territory. I remember when I became pregnant with my daughter the battle was fierce from the beginning. I scheduled a prenatal visit at a local clinic in walking distance from my home. I arrived at the appointment and had taken numerous tests and was given a date to return for follow-up and review of the results. I remember that visit quite well. All who have been to the doctor knows the drill. Your told "Undress and the Doctor will be with you in a moment" I waited, was examined and then told the results were in and things were looking a bit grim. The doctor said I had an extremely significant chance of having a child with Down syndrome. My chances were greater than the average woman of 35. I heard what the Doctor said but I refused to grasp it. I couldn't clutch those words like a pearl or a gem of value because I rebuked it the moment I recognized it was a dart that had been thrown and my armor had shielded me from sustaining injury. My shield of faith immediately began combating the stench of fear that wanted so badly to consume the room and over take me. The words were putrid and I shut them down. I replied "I heard what you said; I'm not interested in discussing that further what does the other tests say?" This doctor looked at me like I had three heads. She got up with a bit of attitude. I hadn't said anything wrong. I hadn't snarled at her or spoken unkind. Immediately after she walked out the room and closed the door I got up off that table and laid hands on the documents in the chart. I bound up every plan of the enemy and stood on Job 22:28 that I will be able to decree a thing and it be established. I decreed healing because Jehovah-Rapha is our healer and the fetus in my womb was whole. In that doctor's office during those very moments I began re-adjusting the armor I had put on that morning. I began to make sure that my helmet was pressed down and fitting snug. I shifted my breastplate a bit. I tightened my belt and the laces on my shoes. I put some Vaseline on my face and I was ready for battle. I put up my shield and was prepared to wield my sword! The doctor returned with more attitude than I liked but I endured the visit. She wanted to delve back into the severity of what she thought was my circumstance. Little did she know I had given it to Jesus it was now His circumstance.

"... This is what the Lord says to you: Do not be afraid or discouraged because of this vast enemy. For the battle is not yours, but God's."
II Chronicles 20:15

I politely shared again, I heard every word she had said but I did not need her to reinforce it. Her anger was kindled far greater. She actually began to throw a bit of a fit. I did not allow her behavior to shift my stance. I was able to perceive then it wasn't her that was angry it was a force of old. It wanted to grip me with fear. I chose to believe the word of the Lord. Once I was able to get out of her office I went downstairs asked for a transfer of my records to a facility that could better help my circumstances. I knew I could not continue to see this doctor if I wanted to survive this attack and if the baby in my womb was to overcome. This doctor was a faith killer and she was on an assignment. I am aware in the natural she was doing her job. I'm sure she meant me know harm in helping me understand the challenge I faced. I also had to do my job and stand on God's word by any means necessary! I had to walk by faith and not by sight.

I registered for my visit at the new location and because of what was currently in my records I was labeled high risk and had to go to the high risk prenatal department. There was a giant sign on the entry of the door. I wasn't the only one who was facing some form of challenge for the life inside of their womb. I knew I had the weapon of prayer on my side. Oh, the power of prayer, "No one is a firmer believer in the power of prayer than the devil. Not that he practices it, but he suffers from it."[1] I believe in putting prayer into practice and I walked it out daily with great fervor. I continued to offer up sweet incense each day.

The various doctors, specialists, and nurses at St. Luke Roosevelt Hospital were wonderful. They were always optimistic in their approach. Whenever you are facing any kind of hardship you must be around optimistic people if you are determined to overcome. It's a harder journey around those who are pessimistic though not impossible but why take the chance? After several visits one of the medical specialists found what appeared to be a whole around the baby's heart. I went through a barrage of tests and sonograms but I didn't change my view. I believed like the Shunamite woman "It shall be well." (II Kings 4:23)

I love how God will always leave a witness to your testimony and will provide like minded believers who can touch and agree with you. My husband had to work and my friend Angel accompanied me to my scheduled visit with a sonogram specialist. We prayed, touched and agreed before we entered the room. As I lay upon the table I praised God and told Him not my will but His. Whatever He did was just fine because He is the creator and I know He will not put more on me than I can bear and that He will not forsake or leave me. Whatever the outcome I knew and trusted that God would make a way for my husband and I to care for this child. The specialist took a look for what the other doctor saw, her exact words were "Well it must have disappeared, there is nothing present that is abnormal." I had to behave civilized I was in a confined room and it took everything I had in me not to shout. Tears rolled down my face because God is faithful. I was immediately taken out of high risk but the devil had not given up. During delivery I had to have a cesarean section because my daughter' umbilical cord was wrapped around her neck then looped around her leg. I know my husband was praying like never before as he held my hand. We never doubted Gods ability but gave it to Him totally. Despite every attack sent our way God showed His power to save on every side. My daughter was born healthy and sharp as whip. I'm telling you God is able! Our prayer's to God is like sweet incense waffling up. Pray on every stench the enemy tries to bring into your life.

** PRAY AND WATCH **

"There is a way that seems right to a man, but in the end it leads to death."
Proverbs 14:12

We know satans mighty weapon is enticing many to sin and he has a way of dialing down its consequences. He tries to cloud our judgment so that the temptation of sin engulfs us slowly. The act of sin has become greatly tolerated from the pulpit, through the pews to the exit. The word of God's correction isn't magnified like it used to be. Those who are not studious in the learning of the word for themselves will not be in the know. There are some preachers that are simmering in hidden sin and they lie through their lips to justify and cover their un-integrous dealings. The stench of sin is alive and well in Christendom. I have seen, heard and experienced some unsavory things. Sin has a foul odor that is devastating the body of Christ and it is increasingly pouring out of the pores of the pulpits into the pores of the pews. Church leadership is falling left and right. The stench rolls in high tide waves at noon every Sunday. It has become a repetitive cycle that comes through the church doors back into the pews and swishes into the pulpit again. The land has become a barren marsh lacking any form of accountability. The Christian divorce rates are increasing at greater degree than ever before. What are we to do? We are to pray and praise God for the leadership that is holding true. We are to pray and praise God for the churches that are standing solid on true doctrine. We are to pray and praise God for Christ minded believers who want to do better to be better. We are not to lose sight and we are to continue to pray and praise God. He is all knowing (omniscient) and His judgment is certain.

If we find ourselves in a place where the fruit is not growing neither does any remain, we have to exercise wisdom and pray. Seek out a place where life is resilient and recognize a grave yard for what it is. The stench of a grave yard is a tell tale sign. If you remain in the graveyard how long before death consumes you? We are required to worship God in spirit and in truth and to put on the whole armor of God. We are to be professors of the faith that are true possessors of His Holy Ghost Power! Jesus Christ is calling us to a higher level of living. It is by his mercy and grace we can be bathed and cleansed washing away the malodorous stench of sin today. He is returning for church that exudes a pleasant fragrance. He has declared the gates of hell shall not prevail against it. Let's be more like Jesus. He is a sweet and pleasant fragrance.

"Finally, brothers and sisters, rejoice! Strive for full restoration, encourage one another, be of one mind, live in peace. And the God of love and peace will be with you."
II Corinthians 13:11

-Chapter Eight-

A Sweet Aroma

"Ointment and perfume rejoice the heart: so doth the sweetness of a man's friend by hearty counsel."
Proverbs 27:9

An aroma is a distinctive and usually pleasant or savory smell. I love the fragrance Bijan; it is one of my favorite scents. I purchased a bottle for my husband the moment I smelled the cologne. There aren't many fragrances I've encountered that I love both the male and female versions. I can detect it a mile away. Can you immediately identify if you pass by someone that's peeling an orange what it is without a glance? Or the smell of strawberry perhaps grape if someone has a jolly rancher of either flavor? Well the same pleasantry these scents bring to us should be what our lives exude before God. We should be ambrosial fragrances of sacrifice. We should be the true essence of a pleasant aroma.

Hebrew 13:15 says we should continue to lift up a sacrifice of praise to God from the fruit of our lips. The Lord will immediately detect who we are because our praises are distinctively unique. Our praise and worship carries a sweet aroma up towards the heavenlies. He won't confuse us with anyone else He knows the very count of individual hairs on each of our heads. Our sacrifice of praise is sweet incense unto His nostrils. Christ is the friend that sticks closer than a brother and in His counsel we can always depend.

** THE NOSE KNOWS **

When you enter a fancy department store and head for the designated area where fragrances are kept you find a vast selection of scents with a diversity of prices. There are some extremely high end perfumes available if your money can afford it. Knowing the various concentrations of perfume helps understand the cost that may be more affordable for your purse or wallet. There is perfume extract, perfume, Esprit de parfum- a seldom used strength, Eau de parfum, Eau de toilette, Eau de cologne, Perfume mist, and splash or aftershave. Perfume types reflect the concentration of aromatic compounds in a solvent. Perfume oil, ethanol and a mix of water in various percents and volumes determine its value. The high end level of fragrance starts with a percentile of thirty and the more common and least expensive fragrances a percentile of one to three percent. That's a pretty huge drop in the percentage of its purity. Clive Christian Imperial Majesty is the most expensive bottle of perfume in the world and will cost you at least two hundred and fifteen thousand dollars last time I googled it. The bottle is fabulous this is pure perfume at its best. The common cost of perfume can run under fifty dollars and is normally called Eau de toilette or toilet water you won't find "Imperial Majesty" in that category there is no need to look.

Now understanding that there are various concentrations of perfume and the concentration determines the price. If we

A SWEET AROMA

had to measure up between the common and the elite prices of perfume what kind of bottle would you be? Anyone that knows me can attest I have so many bottles of perfume I have to stack boxes in my closet because my dresser has no room. I love the various shapes and designs of the bottles. Some I have only worn once and others I have had to replace because I use them frequently. With all of those bottles I can't tell you that I am actually a fan of each scent. I may like the outside appearance but the fragrance leaves much to be desired. We should all pray that our fragrance sits high on the rector scale in pleasing God. However, if it does not we need to return to our perfumer Christ and have some ingredients added and modified.

A perfumer is also called "a nose" they have the ability to create great fragrance compositions. One would have to also have great odor memory and be able to differentiate hundreds of odors with great precision. Spiritually speaking the various fragrances on the department store shelf of the believer should be love, integrity, patience, enthusiasm, benevolence, forgiveness, generosity, patience, honor, gentleness, hospitality, self-control, and gratefulness, We could also add attentiveness, sensitivity, obedience, thoughtfulness, compassion, meekness, dependability, virtue, endurance and a vast array of others. I'm sure you could list quit a few that have not been listed. Each fragrance should be available in its purest form. We may have some eau de toilette in some fragrances in our coming to Christ but we should be progressively working to get to the one hundred percent because ninety nine and a half won't do.

We are to be mindful that our body, not the church building is the true temple of the living God. We are to respect this temple with great diligence because it is the place where the Holy Spirit takes residence when we give our lives to Christ. This spirit that dwells so richly within us is the only way that we can become capable of producing every fragrance listed above in its purest form. Without the Holy Spirit and the shed blood of Christ this would not and could not become the state of a believer. Is the fragrance called "You" exuding therapeutic aromas that the tired and weary would consider your presence aromatically pleasant? Could they find an encouraging word that rolls off your lip providing the scent of milk and honey? Or do you spew bitter vinegar and discord producing a vile odor? An ambrosial fragrance should be the air circulating from the aura of a Christian.

** THE APOTHECARY **

"And thou shalt make it an oil of holy ointment, an ointment compound after the art of the apothecary: it shall be an anointing oil."
Exodus 30:25

In the bible we are introduced to the work of an apothecary. During the time of Moses God gave him the responsibility

A SWEET AROMA

of overseeing and supervising the creation of an exclusive holy oil to be made specifically for the tabernacle. This oil was to be set apart and was not granted for any other use. An Apothecary is defined in modern times as a druggist or pharmacist. In addition to the holy oil that was exclusive the Apothecary actually, prepared all of the medicines, oils and aromatics mentioned in the Bible. Many of these mixtures were more valuable than gold and silver. The oils that were prepared in the thirtieth Chapter of Exodus were used to consecrate the various articles used in the temple of worship including the ark of the testimony. Anyone that tried to duplicate the mixture given to Moses would be cut off from their people.

"37 And as for the perfume which thou shalt make, ye shall not make to yourselves according to the composition thereof: it shall be unto thee holy for the Lord. 38 Whosoever shall make like unto that, to smell thereto, shall be cut off from his people."
Exodus 30 37-38

The greatest apothecary, perfumer and aroma-therapist already lead the way for each of us to be able to mix a sweet savory of smell. It only requires being before God and remaining in His bosom. This particular mixture is also set apart but was meant for duplication. Jesus is in the mixture, He is the true fragrance wear it well!

** HUMILITY BEFORE PROMOTION **

"I beseech you therefore, brethren, by the mercies of God, that ye present your bodies a living sacrifice, holy, acceptable unto God, which is your reasonable service."
Roman 12:1

When we offer ourselves as living sacrifices we must understand that a sacrifice is that which is devoted to God. So we must transform and conform to the things of God through spiritual discipline. Offering oneself means we are dedicating our lives on the brazen altar freely of own free will. It is a total surrender of oneself a submission of our whole being mind, body and soul. When we are placed in the fire we will surely come forth like pure gold. (Job 23:10) We must entrust our lives to Christ and be willing to put it to service for God and His Kingdom. This is a requirement in the making of a true Christian disciple. It's more than just an outside job. It has to go beneath the epidermis, under the dermis and deeper than the layer called the hypodermis. It must be at the core of our being allowing our pores to exude a sweet and pleasant fragrance.

Humility is a simple willingness to be obedient to God no matter what the personal cost. How sweet the smell of humility. It is the complete surrender and trust that allows a person to lay themselves on the altar, refusing to succumb to anything other than Gods will for their lives. Our motives in seeking God should be pure. You cannot fool the God that is Omniscient. He has already informed you that He knows our thoughts afar off. (Psalm 139:2) Yet there are many people that seek God out for their own gain like He isn't aware. There are people that call on Him only when they have a need or find themselves in trouble. It's clear they lack an understanding. We must not ask the question "what can God do for me?", but live a life inquiring "what can I give to God today with my life?" We are required to exude a pure fragrance of true service. What a pleasant scent in the nostrils of our maker.

** POLLUTION IS NOT AN OPTION **

"Dead flies cause the ointment of the apothecary to send forth a stinking savor: so doth a little folly him that is in reputation for wisdom and honor."
Ecclesiastes 10:1

Do not waste time and energy with things that do not benefit growth. One foolish act or deed can go viral on the internet and ruin one's reputation. A smeared name is hard to erase it takes extensive repair. Sometimes even that is not enough for restoration. We should take note that "The more delicate the perfume, the more easily spoiled is the ointment. Common oil is not so liable to injury. So the higher a man's religious character is, the more hurt is caused by a sinful folly in him."[1] God has a standard for us to live by. Our very thoughts and actions should hold to those standards. Every believer is cautioned to guard their heart with all diligence. (Proverbs 4:23) Be the pleasant aroma you're called to be you cannot afford contamination.

Facts surrounding gravity makes it clear that an object can only stay in the air for a limited time before having to come down. If a man puts you in a high place he can change his mind and put you in a low place. When God sets you high no man can pull you out of your place. The sun, moon and stars are up high in the galaxy. They have been defying gravity before the beginning of time. How? It is by God's power through His spoken Word. Each one rests obediently in their place just as He has ordained it to be.

Let your aroma be a soothing incense to Gods nostrils all you have to do is stay low to remain high. Just stay low at Gods feet and He will raise you up. Like the sun, moon and stars He will allow gravity to be defied for you too, God will grow you like the beautiful night blooming Jasmine. Your aroma will exude far beyond your immediate sphere. The night blooming Jasmine's smell is sweet and strong. It requires little care from man. No man can share the glory for what God wants to do through and for you. I hope you aspire to be a servant fit for the master's use. Walk with a spirit of obedience to His will seeking to serve rather than be served. Jesus provides a sound place in an unstable world. Even when you find circumstances which you face to be a bit tumultuous on this life's journey, stay at his feet. Worldly pollution and contamination is not an option.

** LIVING LIFE LIKE ITS GOLDEN **

"A word fitly spoken is like apples of gold in pictures of silver."
Proverbs 25:11

We always hear people refer to an apple having been eaten by Adam and Eve as the fruit that lead to the fall of man. There is nothing in the Word of God that clarifies what kind of fruit it actually was. However if it were indeed an apple thank God for the Golden apple in Jesus. Take a bite out of life everlasting and live your life like its golden. Let the sweet savor of the golden apple waffle up out of your pores. Let your belly be full of the golden apple until it pours out on the people you meet. Let your house be built of savory goods that produce pleasant aromas. Let your house contain pleasantry that when it is encountered by those who are hungry and lost in the wilderness of life they can be fed. When there is a Hansel and Gretel in the forest if your house is the first they come upon let this house be a gateway to Christ. Let the trees in the forest shine brightly with golden apples dangling from their branches. Don't allow your house to be a witch haven that leads to eternal

damnation but a place that leads to a life changing destination that is heaven bound. Your outer glow should be visible and an abundance of delightful sweets should exude a pleasant fragrance unto the nostrils of God and man. Your house should be full of delectable pastries from golden cookies to golden yellow cake on the rooftop.
Let the true manna from God be the golden bread in your heart.

As believers we should always walk upright. We are walking epistles being read by men daily. In every step we take we are representing and showing forth the Christ in us. Let us live life like it is golden. We should always have a golden apple pie to give freely to a stranger as we pass by in the form of a smile. We should willingly share a golden graham cracker smore through a kind word spoken. Allow the savory aroma of a golden nugget to roll right off your tongue to encourage and edify. When there are people around that we know are in need we should share a few of our golden chocolate coins that they are made wealthy in love. Let the sweet fragrance that exudes so fragrantly from our pores cause them to seek the God of our salvation.

> "Give and it will be given to you. They will pour into your lap a good measure- pressed down, shaken together, and running over. For by your standard of measure it will be measured to you in return."
> Luke 6:38(NIV)

A SWEET AROMA
.....................μγμ........................

The word declares the same measure that we use in our giving that God will allow it to return to us in the very same measure. I pray you let your measure be golden. Kick back grab some golden grapes, and bask in the sweetness of God's love. Enjoy Christ as the ultimate golden caramel and live life like its golden.

> *"Oh taste and see that the Lord is good: blessed is the man that trusteth in him."*
> *Psalm 34:8*

Let your life arise unto God's nostrils with a golden scent! In Christ you can and you should live life like its golden. Enter into a wealthy place in Jesus it certainly exceeds more than a fat paycheck, a huge 401(k) account, a luxury car or a mansion that sits on a hill. Your life can be better, and you can be happier, without any of these material possessions. All you need to start living life like its golden is a personal and intimate relationship with Jesus Christ as it has already been stated. Every single one of us has the power of choices to determine what will make us confident and happy. However, without Christ at the forefront it will never amount to anything that will last.

In Christ you are able to discover the purpose of your life. Knowing your purpose will give you more confidence to live life like its golden. You will be able to stand firm in who you are and whose you are in this world without compromise or regret. You can live life like its golden having authentic integrity and infinite possibilities. In Christ we can stand in truth with clarity and undeniable conviction! Live your life like it's golden. Look inward for your truth because when Christ is the center of your life you become empowered through the Holy Spirit to do greater works than Christ did when he was in the earth realm.

> *"12 I tell you the truth, anyone who has faith in me will do what I have been doing. He will do even greater works, because I am going to the Father. 13 And I will do whatever you ask in my name, so that the Son may bring glory to the Father"*
> *John 14:12-13 (NIV)*

Grab hold to Jesus Christ let Him saturate you with His presence. Let your total being exude a pleasant fragrance unto the nostrils of a loving God. Let the malodorous stench that was once you; be forever laid to rest in the grave yard never to arise again. In Christ there is a place where you are at liberty to be you. There is a place where you can achieve your full potential and live a life beyond your wildest dreams. You can have victory in every single area of your life. In Christ and in Him only can you expand and reach higher heights. In Him you can live life in the earth realm and life eternal like its golden. Let Christ be in you pores deep; let this be the pleasant fragrance that you exude.

-Notes-

Chapter 1:
1) Blue Letter Bible Lexicon g2588.
2) The KJV New Testament Greek Lexicon, 2588.
3) Sylvia S. Mader, *Human Biology 10th Edition*, (McGraw-Hill Companies 2008), 73.

Chapter 2:
1) Learning to Flee the Lust of the Eyes Sermon, 2009 Quote, John Barnett.
2) David M. Levy, *The Tabernacle: Shadows of the Messiah*, (The Friends of Israel Gospel Ministry, Inc. 1993), 52.
3) John Ritchie, Tabernacle in the Wilderness, Kregel Publications 1982, 103.

Chapter 4:
1) The Science of Smell Part 3: Odor Detection and Measurement, Iowa State University, University extension PM 1963 c, October 2004.

Chapter 6:
1) Death – Definition from Miriam Dictionary Miriam-Webster.com, 2011.

Chapter 7:
1) Quote – Guy H. King

Chapter 8:
1) Jamieson, Fausset & Brown's Commentary, The Zondervan Corporation 1961, Pg. 485.

About the Author:

Dr. Maynard is a charismatic teacher, preacher and sought after Conference speaker proclaiming the empowering message of hope through salvation in Jesus Christ.

Dr. Maynard is the founder and CEO of a network of kingdom focused companies and ministries, including: Global Kingdom Voices, M.G.M. Ministries International, Logos 2 Rhema University and G.K.V. Radio an internet Christian Broadcasting station touching lives near and far, continually expanding through technology to reach the uttermost parts of the earth.

Dr. Maynard holds, a Doctorate in Philosophical Theology, A Doctorate, Masters, and a Bachelors degree in Sacred Theology in addition to a Bachelor of Science in Criminal Justice.

For Booking Contact:
M.G.M. Ministries International
WWW.MGMMinistries.Net
1 - (855) God-Will (463-9455)

Truth Serum Publications

Church Folk Going to Hell in a Hand Basket
Beguiled - From the Pulpit through the Pews to the Exit

A. Davis
D. Lundy, Ph.D.
M. Maynard, Ph.D.

God is returning for a church without spot or wrinkle. The world, its activities, and ideologies have crept into the church and remained. Matthew 6:24 declares "No man can serve two masters: for either he will hate the one and love the other, or else he will hold to one, and despise the other. Ye cannot serve God and mammon."

The biblical truth taught by our church patriarchs and matriarchs has been viewed as antiquated. However, the truth of God concerning holiness and righteous living is still the same yesterday, today and forever more. This book reveals some common errors and scriptural grounds to assist in helping to Get Your House In Order!

ISBN # 978-0-9839280-1-0

Available April 2012